"When I first attended Ron LeGrand's Quick Start Real Estate Boot Camp back in 2009, I saw attendees wearing shirts with Ron's trade-marked quote, 'The less I do, the more I make.' And, throughout the boot camp, I heard Ron referring to this same famous mantra. I read it, I heard it, but I didn't 'get it' initially. How could doing less really increase your income? It wasn't until I attended Ron's Business Management Boot Camp that the light bulb began to come on for me. When Ron said, 'Delegate and get out of the way,' I really started to understand this foundational principal to running a truly successful business. I learned that until you really learn how to systemize and automate every aspect of your business, all you have accomplished is replacing your old job with a new job in your new business—except without automating, your new business is your task master and you end up trying to do all the menial tasks that should be delegated.

One 'a-ha' moment for me was when Ron said, 'Whenever you are performing a task that can be delegated and hired out at a rate of $12 per hour, you are only getting paid $12 per hour.' He called this, 'trading dollars for hours,' which will never take you from the poor house to the rich house. As I listened and learned more from Ron, I really began to understand how Ron gets so much done when he told us that his primary responsibility is to make decisions. That's it. He makes informed decisions by having high-quality people on his team reporting to him the information he requires to decide what courses of actions need to take place to continue to grow his multiple businesses.

Ron inspired me to duplicate this automation and systemizing process in mine and Carol Joy's house buying and selling business. I wanted to run my business just like Ron does. So I set out on a mission to automate everything. With Ron's guidance and teaching, I achieved the goal. I now work in my business only five hours per week. I make decisions on which houses to buy and how much to sell them for. It is now common for my company to buy and sell houses I've never personally seen along with not even meeting the sellers or the buyers. All of my marketing, rehabbing, and day-to-day operations are handled by my team. Thanks to Ron LeGrand, I now run my business instead of my business running me. Within twelve months of beginning to implement Ron's automation strategies, my net annual income tripled to a seven-figure income. Congratulations to my mentor and friend for writing and releasing his latest book, *The Less I Do, The More I Make*. This book has the information that can free you from being a slave to your business, allow you to take as many vacations as you like, and all the while significantly increase your net income.

I'm excited for you as you read this book because you are about to learn how to get your life back and truly have the time to enjoy the fruits of your labor. After all, isn't that what owning your own business is supposed to do? Ron LeGrand is about to show you how you can also experience the joy and benefits of 'The less I do, the more I make.'"

—Jay Conner, The Private Money Authority

"Ron LeGrand's slogan, 'The less I do, the more I make,' is the simplest and most profound advice for any entrepreneur who's serious about creating and growing a real business. Thanks to Ron's advice and guidance, my company grew multifold in two years and was recognized as the thirteenth-fastest-growing company in Houston, Texas. Read the recommendations in this book. And then act on them."

—Lance Edwards, educator and author,
How to Make Big Money in Small Apartments

"Ron taught me deal analyzing, business management, breakdown, delegating, cash flow breakdown . . . He really opened up my eyes!"

—Mark Shymko, Spruce Grove, AB

"I like Ron's anecdotes the best. I like his bluntness and direct manner."

—Edward Payne, Kenner, LA

"I love the way Ron drives the most important steps into you again and again. Stop wasting time! Focus/concentrate on revenue generation."

—Gerry Corraini, Calgary, AB

"I believe it is so important to listen to Ron and his mentors to pick me off the floor and get dusted off and to show me where I'm faulting and holding me accountable. Since the start of my relationship with Ron and his team, I truly know this is the path that I will travel and succeed at, and it's only possible with the support and education of Ron LeGrand. I've never learned so much usable information so quickly. How can I not follow his teachings for life, especially every time I get knocked down? Thanks again."

—Joel Ast, Calgary, AB

"Ron's business management advice has given me the tools to take our business to the next level. Ron is an absolute gem. I feel privileged to have had the opportunity to learn from his thirty-plus years of experience. Ron has again changed my thinking process, and I'm very thankful."

—Judy Green, Edmonton, AB

"I wish I would have met Ron years ago. In the process of getting to Ron, I went through a lot of morons. Now, I need more Ron. My wife and I spent thousands of dollars doing stuff that did not work. In 1991, because of an industrial accident, I was off work for six months. Between a very, very small insurance policy and multiple credit cards, we survived but broke. We made progress slowly until we met Ron. We spent the first six months in the mentorship, getting deprogrammed. Now, with a great mentor, we are on the brink of change—the breakthrough we were looking for for years. Deals are starting to happen. This is very exciting. It is the first time that the light at the end of the tunnel is not a freight train rumbling down on our plans to destroy them."

—Stan Olsen, Edson, AB

"Ron gave us new ideas on automation, our perspective is changed, and we will get results."

—Shane Penner, Calgary, AB

"The best real estate investment course that I have ever purchased. Ron is about educating yourself, not just about motivation. As well, you have Ron's mentoring and ongoing support! Fantastic!"

—Carol Lawrence, Red Deer, AB

"Ron covers topics that are truly related to all investor's businesses. The information was great, and I'm looking forward to going home and implementing and working on my business. Ron delivered a simple, straightforward explanation of the obvious (which is not always obvious)."

—Keith Kittrell, San Antonio, TX

"Thanks to Ron LeGrand's business management advice, I feel 110 percent confident to reach my goals toward financial freedom with the killer instinct and drive to start generating deals as soon as I get back!"

—Phillip B., Jersey City, NJ

"I stopped listening to the morns and listened to more Ron. I got a call from a seller who saw my sign; he called with a 3/2 Cape Cod for sale, needing about $15k in work, owed $50k, asking $80k, and the ARV was $195k. We bought the house using a private lender for $60k, placed a sign outside, and took sealed bids for twelve days. After that time, we accepted a bid 'as is' for $126k. We closed on the property in April and took home a check for $63,875.67. That's only 120 days after we bought the property. Thanks Ron; this is my first junker. This is more than what I used to make on my job all year. God bless you."

—Gilbert Mack, Winchester, VA

"The systems and techniques Ron teaches are easily implemented. He is tireless in his efforts to teach us how to do the real estate business. He is always encouraging and showing us ways to improve our systems to make more money. Ron's teaching is outstanding—the best! No one who wants to be in the real estate investing business should miss any conference that Ron teaches."

—Judy Rothhauser, Bradenton, FL

"Ron's business management is awesome! We are one year into the business of full-time real estate investing—eleven deals so far from rehabs, wholesale flipping, short sales, and even one mobile home. Our lives have been changed forever, and we have Ron to thank for that. We look forward to coming to Ron's event; we need it! It helps us to stay focused and get recharged. I owe it to Ron for the counseling to follow through and the business advice. You had the biggest role in making us successful. In one month, we will have four closings—$143k in cash! When it is all said and done, we will be completely out of debt for the first time in our lives with $78k in cash left over."

—Patrick & Doreen Martin, Spring Hill, FL

"It's simple—when we do as you instruct us to do, we succeed! When we don't follow your advice, we have problems. Ron, please don't ever retire! We need regular doses of you!

—Kathy Chapman, Dayton, OH

"If there is anything lacking or not working like a machine in your business, Ron's business management advice is what you need to succeed."

—Sharon Cooper, Cape Girardeau, MO

"Ron has a common-sense approach that makes what he teaches applicable. Ron's willingness to share his experiences and knowledge has changed our lives."

—Jamie Harrington, Taylorsville, NC

"I love learning from Ron. He is amazing. I will improve my business tenfold because of the event. I have been longing for this kind of information to help manage my business better."

—Jonathan Chapman, Dayton, OH

"Straightforward, to the point, direct, and honest—good ideas sprinkled throughout that are extremely valuable. Nuggets of gold."

—Steve & Sherri, Jarrettsville, MD

"Without a doubt, the easy, concise way Ron presents ideas is spot on. He is a talented, knowledgeable teacher. Your ability to convey complete concepts in such a way that the 'average' person can quickly grasp the concepts that will allow them also to become multimillionaires."

—John McWilliams, Mars, PA

"I'm full of anticipation about my future with Eagle Virtual Assistants. If our future is anything like it's beginning, we are in for an exciting time!

The main two things that have impressed me so far is first, that all the staff are so approachable and eager to help, and second, the VA system is very easy to follow.

I must admit that I was a little apprehensive in the beginning, but after getting a few emails outlining the system, I'm now feeling right at home with it.

Laura has installed in me so much confidence to help me get to the next level that I believe the cost of the VAs will be peanuts compared to the gains.

Finally, because I've just got so tired of trying to do everything myself, working in my business sixty-plus hours a week, and in the end, for the most part just spinning my wheels, what we are embarking on should not only increase my income but allow me to use it on the things that 'count' in my life, including my God and my family. That's a great feeling to have. I've finally committed to this awesome plan and believe the results will come."

—Paul White

"Eagle VA has been such a blessing in putting things on my website and making many calls for me. One deal I can think of is a PATlive lead I sent over to my VA; she called and gathered the needed information. The home is in the middle of a renovation and is in a great location near the river. I closed the deal and took over the debt! I have a lot of interest in the home now. Thank you so much. You all are great!"

—Andrew Schlag, Newburgh, IN

"I'd like to leave a commendation for Eagle VA. I am finding my VA to have the southern charm and graciousness I am learning to anticipate when I come to that area of the country. She also has a very fun telephone demeanor. It is obvious from her call logs that she is working very hard for my benefit, and she has a very fast response time to emails and phone calls from me. Additionally, she has provided some great insight into my decision to change the counties that I am working in. If all goes well, I anticipate upgrading my VA membership and would like her to handle it. I trust that I will have a long, mutually beneficial relationship with Eagle VA because of her."

—Stan Shellum, Sunnyvale, CA

"I cannot find enough excellent words to say about my VA! He is without a doubt the most exceptional VA that I could ever imagine! He is an absolutely perfect fit for me, and we get along famously. I am so thrilled to be working with him in my real estate investing endeavors. He is a jewel—a treasure beyond compare. He's the epitome of all that Ron LeGrand and Global Publishing stand for. I am extremely proud to have him on my team. Thank you from the bottom of my heart for assigning him to me! He is an unbelievable asset. Thanks again for everything."

—Cathy Yost, Cumming, GA

"Here is our first deal!

The lead came through Ron's Virtual Assistant service. They found the lead on Zillow.

They answered yes to lease option. This was a couple of weeks before the Great American Real Estate Summit in Orlando, so I called to verify the information. I sent this lead sheet along with others in for the mentors at the summit to call from the deal room.

The mentors made the call from the summit and were able to set up the appointment for us. When we returned from the summit, I called to confirm the time. I sent emails to the Wolff Couple, my mentors, to confirm the time and the agreement. Everything checked out!

Before the appointment, I received an email from the seller suggesting they will pay their mortgage payment during the lease period if I were to pay them full appraisal price for the property. I couldn't believe it! I sent it to our mentors to make sure I was reading it right. Ron's mentors made themselves available if needed by phone during the appointment. We got to the sellers and took some pictures. It was a beautiful home.

While going over the contract, the husband had some concern about the term. He only wanted a twelve-month term. I wouldn't agree with that. So we left without an agreement and just let them talk it over. The next day they emailed me and said they would do an eighteen-month term with no renewals. I checked with Ron's mentors, and they said go ahead with the deal, so here it is:

Purchase price: $445,000
Lease for eighteen months at $375 to cover taxes and insurance.
It needs no repairs. It's 3,800 sq ft., 4 br/3.5 ba; beautiful home.
Exit strategy is a lease-option buyer.

Lease for $2,875/mo. Sale for $465,000. Get a $20,000 deposit. Do my best to stretch it out to the full eighteen months.

This deal happened due to Ron's whole program. His Eagle VA service sent the lead, the deal room at the summit set the appointment, and the mentoring gave support through many emails and being available by phone.

Thank you all so much for everything you do! It works!"

—Dan Kapornyai, NC

"I've had a great experience working with my Gold Club Virtual Assistant for about a month, and in that time she has been very diligent in searching for leads here in the San Francisco Bay Area. Although it's been a market with tight and very low inventory, she was able to search for viable leads in which most the homeowners were open to hearing about options, lease options, and other ways we could help them to sell their homes. We've had great communications, and she is always upbeat and cheerful in our conversations.

Thanks for all your help along the way."

—Clifford Pong, San Bruno, CA

"This is a testimonial to the VA services you provide. I have been an elite member with your VA service for a little over seven weeks now. I am very pleased with my dedicated assistant. She put in every effort possible to keep me happy and is a very understanding, knowledgeable, and caring professional. All of the FSBOs I talk to who have been sent to me by Jenn have compliments about her personality, great attitude, and professionalism, and I can't agree more. Jenn and

I have good communication, and she will do what it takes to accommodate my requests."

—Leo Cochrane, Garner, NC

"The leads my VA sends are fantastic! Very well done! Thanks for the great work. It is nice to get some 'yeses' on the sheets."

—Charles Adams, Sterling, VA

"Hello,

It is I, Alton Jones, all the way from Long Beach, CA.

Here is a quick testimonial on an appointment with my local assistant Amon Dothard. We have a LOI commitment for a lease with option to buy. The lead was sourced by an Eagle Virtual Assistant. This was a property located in Murrieta, CA, which is in Riverside County. It's a 5-bed/3-bath 2591 sq. ft., and the lot is 7405 sq. ft. I could tell that it was a good lead sheet by the notes and comments the Virtual Assistant made. The seller was very motivated due to an aging mother whom she wanted to relocate closer to family. It was becoming an inconvenience to commute to her mom.

In short, here's the deal: I let Amon work the lead from when we received it from the VA. Amon had just attended Ron's Mastermind Boot Camp and Taking Action and Communication Workshop. Because of the training he received during those events, he was able to close for an appointment using the words and techniques that were taught.

Once at the seller's home, we did a quick walk-through and saw that the home was in great condition. Nothing needed to be done other than an easy wipe down and move in. We sat down with the seller and went through the numbers.

Seller wanted $405k and $50K down and a one-year lease. Using the close I learned from Ron, I asked, 'If you can show me comps to support what you are asking, I would be happy to review them in consideration of my offer.' She could not find them. So at that point we got the price down to $380k with $10k and a three-year lease with the right to extend. We pay $1891.00, which is what she pays to her bank. We get the pay down of the debt to resale as a sandwich lease option for $425k with $30k down and $2,100.00 per month, which equals a $209.00 monthly spread. Not too bad!

But here's where it gets better.

For some reason, she completely opened up to us and indicated that she also had another awesome home in another high-end area they want us to do a short sale on. They owe $660k and are trying to get $450k and resale for $550k. Now I know those short sales can be a hit or miss with banks, but what the heck! I will just outsource the work and wait until the end and $100k for my time.

It just goes to show that you go in with one deal in mind, but you come out with two and any other referrals that they may have. Turns out that the seller knows others like her in the same situation.

Bottom Line:

Deal 1:
$30,000 down, $10,000 to seller
$209 per month over thirty-six months, $7,524
$52,500 backend payoff
Total cash: $80,024.00

Deal 2:
Short sale, six to eight months' time
If all is good, we get an approval for $450,000 from the bank.

We resale on the open market for $550,000.

We make $100,000 give or take closing cost.

The total for both deals is $180,024.00!

This is from one seller, one appointment, one VA, one Wolff Couple and, of course, one Ron LeGrand."

—Alton Jones, CEO, West Coast Home Buyer, LLC

"It's been ten months since I attended your 'Control without Ownership' four-day seminar. It was one of the first steps I used to reinvent myself to this current real estate market that had kicked me so hard in the stomach, so to speak. I knew the old ways of doing real estate I had used in the past had to change if I was to stay in real estate.

I love doing rent to own, also known as lease to own, and rehabbing properties. I was already thinking of ways to get the right marketing and forms system to use in this new market we're in. I saw the writing on the wall. Your ACTS program solved that problem for me.

Since that time, I have done eight ACTS deals. I'm using a virtual assistant, and that system is working great for me.

Attached is a check for $13,250.00, which is the best deal I've done so far. I also received $1,000 from the tenant buyer to take the property off the market until closing, for a total of $14,250.00 after expenses!

Ron, I know you like to say I'm old as dirt, but I reinvented myself to this market with the best of the young studs! Thanks for your help!"

—Ray Ritchie, Landis, NC

"Having a VA has opened up a whole new world to my real estate investing business. For minimal time on my part, I receive an abundance of leads. After the lead sheets come in, all I have to do is call the seller with a few follow-up questions and then set a time to meet. I'm in my third month of having a VA. I still have a full-time job, and when I signed up for VA services my immediate goal was to generate enough 'side income' from real estate investing that my wife would no longer have to work (so she can do what she wants—be a stay at home Mom and be my part-time assistant). We are on track to meet this goal, and I should be out of my full-time job within a few months.

My VA, Kayla Baker, has been awesome to work with. Every week on Tuesdays at 8:30 we have our weekly call, and she is always in a great mood. Whether I call or e-mail her with a question or comment, she always gets back to me right away—she is an invaluable part of my real estate investing business.

So far, I've only had Eagle VA assist with calling FSBOs, and I look forward to soon having Eagle VA assist with manning my website and posting ads for me. I just can't say enough great things about Eagle VA!"

—Tony Anczer, Dyer, IN

"The Virtual Assistant service has been reliable and consistent. The VA personnel are knowledgeable in obtaining sellers' information, and all sellers' leads have been processed in a timely manner. The weekly status and update calls are very beneficial in deal flow management."

—Marvin Taylor, VA

"Thank you, Gold Club Virtual Assistants.

After signing up, our assigned VA contacted us and introduced herself, and the rest is history. We are grateful to have such a quality individual as part of our team who is responsive and adaptive to our requirements.

She manages our lead flow of potential sellers and buyers and makes the appropriate follow-up calls. Knowing that she is handling this part of our business leaves us the time to focus on making decisions and closing deals.

A big 'thank you' to her and the VA team for making our jobs easier. Keep up the great work!"

—John Martin & Amy Hinderer

"It has been our pleasure to work with the Eagle Virtual Assistants since we joined the Masters program in April 2014. They are professional and persistent in calling day after day and following up on prospects until they acquire a lead sheet or exhaust the possibility. We even moved during that time, requiring them to change the location of their calls from one state to another and then back again, which they did with no problem.

Ariel McNeil has been the lead VA working with us for many months, and we appreciate her attention to our needs and responsiveness to our requests. Her consistent communication with us gives us confidence in what they are doing daily on our behalf.

The Eagle VAs are trained extremely well to make the first contact with a prospect a pleasant and professional one. We would recommend them and their service to anyone with a need for lead generation."

—Tim & Dawn Glass

THE LESS
I DO,
THE MORE
I MAKE

THE LESS
I DO,
THE MORE
I MAKE

AUTOMATE or DIE...

*How to Get More Done in Less Time
and Take Your Life Back*

Ron LeGrand

Published by Advantage, Charleston, South Carolina.
Member of Advantage Media Group.

ADVANTAGE is a registered trademark and the Advantage colophon is a trademark of Advantage Media Group, Inc.

Printed in the United States of America.

ISBN: 978-1-59932-711-2
LCCN: 2016933073

This publication is designed to provide accurate and authoritative information in regard to the subject matter covered. It is sold with the understanding that the publisher is not engaged in rendering legal, accounting, or other professional services. If legal advice or other expert assistance is required, the services of a competent professional person should be sought.

Advantage Media Group is proud to be a part of the Tree Neutral® program. Tree Neutral offsets the number of trees consumed in the production and printing of this book by taking proactive steps such as planting trees in direct proportion to the number of trees used to print books. To learn more about Tree Neutral, please visit **www.treeneutral.com**. To learn more about Advantage's commitment to being a responsible steward of the environment, please visit **www.advantagefamily.com/green**

Advantage Media Group is a publisher of business, self-improvement, and professional development books and online learning. We help entrepreneurs, business leaders, and professionals share their Stories, Passion, and Knowledge to help others Learn & Grow. Do you have a manuscript or book idea that you would like us to consider for publishing? Please visit **advantagefamily.com** or call **1.866.775.1696.**

DEDICATION

This book is not dedicated to any one person. It's dedicated to all of the hardworking, small entrepreneurs who made this country great and continue to do so. As I go through life and come in contact with these entrepreneurs in multiple different businesses, I find they all have the same problem, and it bothers me to see most of them going through their entire business career and never fixing that problem. Of course, that problem is they spend way too much time working *in* their business and never really dedicate enough time working *on* their business.

I wrote this book for those entrepreneurs in a hope that I can play some small part in fixing the bad habits they have accumulated over the years, and maybe, just maybe, there are one or two things in this book that will relate and get implemented and begin the process of change—change from being a job slave, even if you are the boss, to a business owner. Believe me, that is a big change.

The purpose of a business is only one: take care of its owners. It's not to have a place to report to work every day and spend all of your waking hours trying to make a living. It's to take care of the owners. All of the other things that come along with the business are benefits, not the purpose for being in business.

I'm dedicating this book to all of those business owners who probably should take more time to take care of themselves and build a business that can do that even when they decide they don't want to work at it anymore.

There are so many people in my life who allow me to live every day without having to be any one place at any one time that I couldn't possibly mention them all, but there is one person I must mention here, and that is my wife, Beverly. On September 18, 2015, we were married fifty years—a span of time over which we produced four children, nine grandchildren, and nine great-grandchildren, at least as of this writing. The number tends to continue growing.

During that entire fifty years, Beverly has never worked in my business. I always say that's likely why we've been married so long. She says it's because I'm away a lot. She has stood by and watched me make multiple mistakes, some of them gigantic in size and costing a lot of money for my training. Of course, she's always had an opinion but never to the point where it interfered with anything I chose to do in my multiple ventures.

Frequently she told me I was doing the wrong thing, and looking back, darned if she wasn't right almost every single time, so over the years, I've learned to listen to her. Of course, that doesn't mean that I take her advice. After all, I am a man, but I can tell you after so many blunders when she says, "It won't work," it causes me to stop and think and more carefully analyze everything that I do. I don't know what it is about women, but they have this uncanny sense, and guys, if you're reading this, you probably ought to listen to them more.

We've been through a lot together, so much it would have to be the subject of another book, and I wouldn't trade it for any of my accomplishments, any money I've made, or any other relationships that I have. So this book is dedicated to all of the hardworking entrepreneurs but also to their spouses who make it easier and more fun to do the things we do.

TABLE OF CONTENTS

FOREWORD

I could call my early real estate investing career "Confessions of a Control Freak," or "How Ron LeGrand Saved My Sanity!" Hi, my name is Brian Wolff, and I'm a control freak.

It's always been a struggle for me to let go, and real estate investing was no different. I created every marketing piece, took every phone call, showed up at every meeting, and completed all the paperwork. I did it all. I even did all my own closings with a notary at the bank!

Thank heavens we met Ron LeGrand in 2002, and his famous homespun pearls of wisdom fell upon my eager ears, "The Less I Do, The More I Make!" Through those eight simple words and the training that followed it, Ron LeGrand changed our lives forever.

My lovely wife, Lynette, and I had been around real estate for decades, but this was a new concept to us. When we met Ron, we were absolutely not looking to just trade one rat race for another. We were both already working over fifty hours per week. Being from the Great Midwest (Minnesota), family was always number one with us. Between us we have thirteen sisters and brothers and three great kids of our own. Our dearest desire was to be able to spend a lot more time with our family, without sacrificing our lifestyle. That meant getting all the necessary action steps done while using as little of our own time and energy as possible.

So we had to figure out exactly what Ron meant with his famous yet enigmatic saying.

I turned it over and over in my mind, searching for hidden meaning. I knew Ron meant that applying automation to our investing business would free us up to close more deals, thereby making a lot more money. He meant that we should be focusing on the big picture, not the minutia. He meant that any time we could get somebody else to do something for us, let them do it!

But then I went deeper. It occurred to me that it really comes down to another real estate concept that Ron had also imparted to us, "Highest and Best Use." That phrase typically applies to land usage in commercial deals, but doesn't it also apply to time management and division of labor? Ron taught us that we needed to do what we do best, and let others do the rest.

Ron knows what his students want and need. That's why he and his terrific company Global Publishing, Inc., headed up by the awesome Jennifer Shedlin, have developed powerful systems to automate his investing students. He has marketers, answering services, automated voice recorders, mentors, and a trained team of virtual assistants to take care of every aspect of our businesses. All are tried and true, so we can rely on them with peace of mind. I finally knew I could let go of the control because a wiser mind had set up a winning system of delegation.

Through the intelligent application of automation, Ron freed us to succeed. Now we can focus on the highest and best use of our time—decision making, closing calls, and deal meetings. Following Ron's guidance, now we've even delegated most of those! Together, we spend less than five hours per week in our real estate investing business; and with Ron's systems in place, we have become multimillionaires.

That is the glory of automation. It all comes down to this: *automation equals freedom!* The whole point is that you can spend a lot more time *doing what you want, when you want.* Ron gave us the goal—to have a lot of money coming in, with little time and energy going out. Now he and Global Publishing have the structure in place to help new investors execute this plan, and we hope you are one of them. You'll find Ron and us at Global Publishing's events, at which he will teach you, too, the true meaning of "the less I do, the more I make." Thank you, Ron—you changed our lives and our family's lives forever. We would never be where we are without you and your powerful systems!

Enthusiastically Yours,
Brian & Lynette, the Wolff Couple!

About the Author

Ron LeGrand has been an entrepreneur from the age of eighteen. During his lifetime, seventy years as of the writing of this book, he's really only had three jobs, one of which was for his dad, Frenchy LeGrand, when Ron was in his teens. At the age of eleven, Ron's dad put him to work on the boardwalk in Jacksonville Beach, Florida, where he owned a lot of rides and games. He worked about twelve hours per day, seven days per week for $20 per week, which he spent in about twenty minutes. But during that time, he learned the meaning of work. In fact, he came to understand work as one of the fundamental reasons for living—a key to one's self-esteem and ability to get through life and achieve big things.

Fresh out of high school, Ron went to work at a service station, his second job, and worked there for several years before actually becoming a manager of a Standard Oil station, which would remain his career for the next ten years.

In 1965, one hot afternoon as he came out of his class to go to his car in the parking lot, Ron discovered there were three people in his car, his best friend (Carl Guest) and two other ladies. One of those ladies happened to be Beverly, who soon became his wife and has been for more than fifty years.

Shortly after graduating from high school in 1965, Ron moved to Springfield, Ohio, where his wife is from, and for two years worked at International Harvester Company, which was considered the best job in town at that time. He often says, "It was the most boring job of my life. They could have trained a monkey to do what I did." And for that reason and none other, he decided to quit that great job at the end of two years and go back to the service station, taking a big pay cut. Once you have the mind of an entrepreneur, it's very difficult to swap hours for dollars, especially when your entire day is dedicated to learning more jokes and watching the clock.

For the next ten years, Ron managed his own service station in Springfield, Ohio, before it occurred to him that he wasn't built for the cold weather, being a Florida boy. He moved his entire family back to Jacksonville, Florida, where he was born and has lived there ever since.

In 1982, a washing machine changed Ron's life. He was working at a service station as a partner but barely making a living. One day, when he came home from work, Beverly told him that the washing machine was broken and asked him to buy her a new one. An argument ensued, lasting into the evening, and both went to bed upset. It was the middle of the night when he woke up and realized, "What an idiot. You've been married for seventeen years, you have four children, and you can't even buy your wife a washing machine to wash your clothes." It was at that turning point where he decided something had to change. He had no intentions of going through the rest of his life living from day to day, not even putting enough money aside to buy groceries for a full week but having to go to the grocery store every other day.

It was then Ron saw an ad that said, "Come learn how to buy real estate with nothing down and no credit." Of course, that appealed to him because he had neither of those. On March 12, 1982, he attended his first real estate seminar because it was free. At that seminar, he was convinced to pay $450 to attend a two-day seminar coming up the next weekend, but unfortunately, he didn't have the money. He went to a couple of friends, though, and borrowed the money and made it to that two-day seminar, a life-changing event he's looked back on ever since.

Most of the information provided during that seminar went right on by and over Ron's head. He had no experience in real estate whatsoever and didn't understand 90 percent of what the instructor was saying. However, he did pick up one technique that he used to go out and make his first $3,000 check within three weeks, and of course, that was the beginning of a whole new lifestyle. He immediately called his boss and quit his job, with nothing to fall back on. There was no savings account, no IRA, no wife working, and no one to borrow money from if he got in a pickle. What he did have was the entrepreneurial spirit and the confidence to know that he could make a better living, as well as the freedom along the way to enjoy it.

Before long, Ron was doing deal after deal after deal. In his first two years, he had amassed more than two hundred units of apartments and houses, all low-income stuff that he had learned to buy and sell within his comfort zone. However it didn't take long to figure out that all he had done was build a big mess, buying the wrong houses in the wrong areas for the wrong reasons simply because he could do it without using his money or credit. It took five years to clean up the mess he had made in his first two. He was seven years into the business before he discovered how to turn single-family houses into cash flow instead of into tenants running his life.

As time went on, Ron began building systems, and over the years, they have become the standard in the industry. There has never been a time when it is easier to buy and sell houses without risk than today—all because of Ron's systems.

After a few years of Ron's buying and selling houses at a rather rapid pace, people started coming to him and asking, "Can you show me how to do this?" It didn't take him long to figure out, "Gosh,

I'm saying the same things over and over again. I might as well put it into a seminar and see if people will pay me to hear what I have to say," and thus he did. His first seminar cost $10 to attend, and the room was full. Immediately, he knew, "Gosh, people will pay me," and he scheduled the next seminar. This time, however, the price was $395 for a two-day event. Sure enough, they came. Oh, a lot fewer of them, but still they came. That was the beginning of Ron's entire information-marketing business, which today is a multimillion-dollar annual business under the umbrella of Global Publishing, Inc., in Jacksonville, Florida, a company with more than fifty employees.

Ron has created numerous home-study courses on just about every subject you can think of concerning real estate, as well as others, and he still does live training in four-day events under the name "Quick Turn Real Estate School" somewhere around the country almost every month. Global delivers one-on-one mentoring and other services, including virtual assistant services for all of its clients. All of this because of a washing machine.

Over the years, Ron became an exceptional platform speaker and then began teaching others to do the same. Yes, he is personally responsible for most of the current real estate gurus becoming gurus. They started in his classes, learning the business, and then he helped them learn how to teach the business and start their own information-marketing companies. Some call him Papa. Others call him Moses because of his long tenure in the business. He has shared the platform with the best of the best, including past presidents, movie stars, military heroes, billionaires, multimillionaires, business stars, actors, and famous people of all types. In fact, he has hired several of them to speak for him at his annual real estate summits, the likes of Dr. Phil, Jay Leno, Henry Winkler, Terry Fator, Jerry Rice, Don Shula, and many others.

Ron's highest-grossing speech produced $459,000 in ninety minutes, not from a speaker's fee but the sales spurred from the platform, an art he has mastered over the years. Ron doesn't collect a speaker's fee. He actually generates revenue for the promoter, and usually they split the proceeds.

Over the years, he's had several businesses, as he is a firm believer in multiple income streams. These businesses include restaurants, information-marketing companies, real estate firms, membership programs, real estate development projects, coaching, consulting, mastermind groups paying upward of $25,000 per member, and a few others.

He will be the first to confess that he didn't always understand or implement this thing called automation. In fact, it's only in the past few years that it has become a focus of all his businesses, as he works at getting them to run without his presence. That's what this book is all about. Once Ron's internal switch turned on and he went from everyday minutia to everyday management, things started turning quickly. Having time to work *on* your business instead of *in* your business will make it grow very quickly. Ron can attest to the fact that this strategy works in any business, as you will discover in this book.

INTRODUCTION

Are You Feeling the Pain?

Take Your Business— and Life—Back

The title of this book is *The Less I Do, the More I Make*. What does that mean? Well, it doesn't mean the less you work, the more money you earn. It means, the less you work *in* your business, the more you can work *on* your business, improving it and providing a more rewarding lifestyle for you and your family.

Over the last forty-five years, I've run multiple businesses simultaneously—I still do. Over three decades, I've taught hundreds of thousands of people how to buy and sell houses without using their own money or credit, and simultaneously, I had to teach them how to run a business.

Learning real estate is a lot easier than learning to run a business. I see the same mistakes time after time in daily business operation, whether I'm educating longtime business owners, new entrepreneurs, or even so-called "skilled entrepreneurs." It's no mystery why most small businesses fail within their first five years.

Running a business right is not about working hard or long hours. It's about working smart. Unfortunately, most business owners live their entire lives without figuring this out. They never take action to correct the core problem because they don't even know it needs correcting. Do you fall into this category? Are you spending so much time making a living that you can't take the time to get rich?

All of us were raised to be unorganized messes. We were taught from the time we entered school to work hard, put in time, make a living, and be good citizens. However, I would remind you broke people taught us this. Yes, we were trained to be broke our entire lives. Think about it: when you were born, you were handed to a broke nurse. When you left the hospital, you were probably in the presence of your broke parents. When you checked into school, you were taught by broke teachers. Then you went to high school to be taught by more broke teachers. If you went to college, you were taught by broke professors, and all of your working life, it's likely you hung around broke people because they were similar to you, and you felt comfortable associating with people who had very little.

For most employees, conversations in the workplace revolve around being broke, thinking broke thoughts, taking broke actions, making the mistakes that broke people make, living the lives broke people live. But nothing says you have to remain broke. Being poor is a state of mind. Being broke is a temporary condition.

"Okay, Ron," you're probably thinking, "you're insulting me before I even start reading your book." Well, I hope not. I'm just pointing out a fact. You might be asking, "What does being broke have to do with *The Less I Do, the More I Make*?" The answer is simple. You can't achieve wealth or even financial independence through cash flow by spending every day doing the same things that got you where you are today—less than rich.

If you're not wealthy, there's a reason. A large part of it is likely because you waste time in the same way every day and don't do the things that could make you rich. Instead, you do the things that keep you busy. If that's the case, this book is for you.

I'm a tell-it-like-it-is guy. Honestly, your feelings are not my main concern. If I don't stir up a little controversy and get under your skin from time to time, I won't have your attention long enough to get the message of this book across. If I had to sum that message up in one phrase, it would be pretty simple: *quit working your ass off and start accomplishing something in life.*

There's only one purpose of a business. It's not to take care of employees. It's not to produce a good product or a service. It's not to be of service to mankind. Its only purpose is to take care of its owners. Those other things are benefits but not the purpose of owning a business.

If, in fact, the business does not take care of its owners, it probably can't do any of those other things because the owner is mired in minutia, doing the same things day-in and day-out, spinning wheels like a rat in a cage but getting nothing accomplished. If that describes you or someone you know, you've picked up the right book.

Why do so many businesses fail before they even have a chance to get launched? One big reason is a lack of capital—they're under-capitalized from the start. Many owners grossly underestimate the amount of money it's going to take just to get the business up and running, never mind to reach the break-even point or the point of profitability.

I've had several businesses that would have died an instant death if I hadn't had the capital to support them until they could make a profit on their own.

Another major reason for failure is that some businesses simply start with a lousy product or service. They expect consumers to exchange hard-earned money for that product or service on a regular basis and to keep returning to buy crap.

In my experience, however, the biggest problem causing business failure is the person in charge. Yes, that would be you.

Most people who go into business are pretty good at delivering a product or a service, but they don't take nearly enough time learning how to run a business. They don't perform any due diligence behind the scenes, figuring out what it takes to make the business successful. Eating at restaurants doesn't qualify you to operate one. I know—I have two now, and I've had several others over the years. Business failure is, more than anything, a people problem, and its biggest components are managing time and controlling minutiae.

Business operators get so immersed in day to day operations, addressing one headache after another, that they don't have time for anything else. There's a common mistake I see my students making over and over, and it doesn't seem to matter if they are new or have been around awhile. That mistake is: doing everything they can to feel busy except the critical things required to stay in business! Running a business this way quickly becomes painful. You want to succeed, so the business begins to consume your life. This book holds the secret to taking your business—and your life—back.

Believe me, you can do it if you're willing to change your habits. I went from being an overworked, underpaid auto mechanic to a multimillionaire, but it wasn't easy. I must confess, it took a long time for me to learn the lessons I'm outlining in this book—in fact, close to twenty-five years.

Today, I am a part-time real estate investor and the owner and operator of several businesses, including two restaurants, two information-marketing companies, three consulting companies, and a couple of others. None of these businesses requires my presence to operate, and what little I do contribute is usually by email or phone.

Most of the times I do show up, frankly, my staff probably wishes I would stay home.

I mostly work from the house, but sometimes I show up at the crack of noon. I have only one purpose in my businesses. If you don't get anything out of this book, please get this: your sole function as the owner and operator of a business is to quickly work yourself to the point where the only thing you have to do is . . . *make decisions.*

If you can get yourself to the point where all you do is make major decisions and everything else is done by someone else or outsourced to another company, you'll start to love your business. Imagine running a business that's highly profitable and more than taking care of your personal needs—with hardly any personal participation from you.

This is no exaggeration. It's exactly how my businesses run, but I can't say it was always so. When I started in real estate in 1982, I worked twelve hours a day, seven days a week. Every little thing that had to be done, I thought, could only be done by me. No one else could do it as well. Running my business consumed my entire life. I watched my children grow up without me because I wouldn't take time away from my business. All of my thoughts focused on making more money.

I answered my own telephones. For quite a while, I did my own secretarial work. I drove around looking at every single property I considered buying. I took all the calls from buyers and all the calls from sellers, and I did every other stupid thing that many folks in business continue to waste their days doing.

Over the years, little by little, I learned how to turn loose and delegate. Gradually, I figured out that other people could do anything that I could do, and most of the time, they did it better. I grew to like this plan and the idea that I didn't have to be responsible for every little thing

It wasn't easy. I'm a man, a control freak. It was all I could do to force myself to give up some of the tasks I thought I had to complete. Over time I made myself release larger and larger jobs. Eventually, I realized, "By golly, they are getting it done without me." In fact, I sometimes got upset the world kept spinning without my participation.

I started learning what the words "automation" and "systemization" mean. I implemented small procedures to relieve the pressure from the minutia. We implemented more, and then over time, we created our own systems because we couldn't find anything out there that would work for us. The poet William Blake said, "I must create a system or be empowered by another man's," and I have taken those words to heart. Today, any business I'm a part of is systemized and automated, and I wouldn't have it any other way.

This, my friend, is why I chose to write this book. This message is too important to keep secret. I want to get it out there to anyone who would like to be an entrepreneur or who already is one. It's highly likely you will make changes in the way you operate your business after reading this book.

Here are just some of the things I'll cover:

- The most common mistakes that lead to failure in business.

- Why your current process isn't working and how to fix it.

- How to change habits and improve organization.

- How to manage your time more effectively.

- How to grow your business painlessly through marketing.

- How to eliminate much of your workload through delegating and outsourcing.

- The online resources that let you get almost any business task done competently and painlessly, for pennies.

The resources in this book alone are worth thousands of dollars to you in saved time. This doesn't even count the additional revenue you'll earn when you discover just how easy it is complete the tasks you have put off or ignored, costing your business money every day.

Before we get to strategies for changing habits, delegating, and outsourcing, we must diagnose the problems holding back your business. In chapter 1 ("How Do You Rate?"), I'll ask you to take a short test to see where you land on the minutiae scale.

Chapter 1

How Do You Rate?

Let Ron Diagnose Your Dilemma

Before we discuss a cure, we have to first diagnose the disease. Let's explore the most common problems in business and how they might relate to you.

The biggest problem in business is that most business owners find themselves working so hard *in* their businesses that they can't take time to work *on* them. This problem manifests itself in various ways, and in my experience, the mistakes are pretty much the same regardless of the product or service. The following test will highlight the specific issues affecting you most. Take a minute to answer these questions honestly, without skipping ahead. Let's see how you rate and whether or not this book applies to your business.

You might think you don't need to take this test because your business doesn't have any serious problems. And yet, there's a reason you're holding this book in your hands, still reading along. If you have one of those mythical, perfect businesses, I sure would like to hear about it because whatever you're doing, I want to do it, too. In the likely event this is not the case, go ahead and take the test. Why not? It only takes a moment, and even if you don't learn anything, it will be fun.

Be honest as you answer questions—and don't worry, no one is grading how well you do. No teacher is present, and you're not in a classroom. For this test, it's just you and . . . you.

Read the following statements and check all that apply to you:

❑ You spend all day getting things done, but at the end of the day, not much has gotten done.

❑ You spend so much time trying to make a living, you can't make any real money.

❑ Your stomach is in knots all the time because you can't ever get to the bottom of your "to do" list. It grows faster than you can check items off of it.

❑ You make promises you can't keep because you forget you made them, and other people's promises go unfulfilled because you both forget them, and no one follows up.

❑ You are making the same amount of money you made several years ago—nothing's changed except that the days get longer, the list gets bigger, and you have less time today than when you started.

❑ Every day is the same-old, same-old—filled with minutiae and never-ending tasks, and you just can't make enough time to get it all done.

❑ Your family feels deserted because even when you're home, you're not home: you are preoccupied with all the junk you have to get done in your business.

❑ You're making a living but not getting rich—and you don't see how you ever will.

❑ You can't imagine how you will ever be able to retire.

❑ You want to accomplish various tasks but can't find the right help.

❑ You have great ideas but can't find the time to implement them, or by the time you try to, they're gone—their time has passed.

❑ You can't travel or take time off without worrying.

❑ Your business is not in a state that would allow you to sell it.

❑ You're aging quickly and don't feel you should have to work this hard at this stage in life.

How did you do? How does your business rate? Scan the list above, and count the number of boxes you checked.

If you checked . . .

- **None.** You're lying. Get real. Nobody's that good. Give this book to a friend in business. It will do you no good.

- **One or two**. You are truly doing well in your business. Congratulations, friend, you're running your business instead of letting it run you.

- **Three or four**. This book could be a big help, allowing you to do more and make more by spending less time working.

- **Five**. This book is not only for you, but reading it should be a priority. Picture the little sign that says, "In case of emergency break glass." This book is behind the glass, friend, and you have an emergency on your hands. The advice in these pages will sound the alarm and provide the help that saves you.

- **Six or more**. Life sucks, but don't worry, you can always serve as a warning to others. No, I am kidding. You are not dead yet, but in all seriousness, the end is near. You are on your way out. There is hope, but you must start focusing on the things in this list that constitute your biggest problems. You must do something on a daily basis to eliminate those issues from your life, or stress could eliminate you.

The secret of my success in multiple businesses—and the secret of this book—is you'll be able to accomplish more and make more if you spend less time doing and more time thinking. Sound irrational? It won't once you understand you are your own worst enemy and most of what you do daily is probably a waste of time, energy, and resources.

The Enemy Is Here; It Is Us

If you are resistant to getting out of your own way, can you honestly say the issues above aren't relevant to you? You and I both know they are. You have some, if not all, of these issues in your business, as most owners and I do, and if you could delegate most of what you're doing now, it would free up your time to focus on growing revenue and wealth and actually enjoying the process because you would no longer be a slave to it. Taking your business—and life—back comes down to changing a few habits, and one of those is to . . .

Start Letting Others Do 90 Percent of What You Currently Do

This is no easy proposition, especially for a man, because, let's be honest, we're all control freaks. Believe me, it took many long years for me to come to the conclusion that I'm really not so important. But what I eventually realized—and hope you will too—is that the methods outlined in this book allow you to delegate and change your process, freeing up more time to focus on decision making and building revenue, which is your proper role in your business. You and only you will stay focused on revenue. You simply can't hire folks who care as much about it as you do.

You're probably thinking, *Shouldn't I be involved in day to day operations? How am I going to run a business without being hands-on?*

That's a very good question, but to answer it, we must first define "hands-on." For me, being "hands-on" means I spend almost all my time doing one thing and one thing only . . . making decisions

I'm a Lazy Entrepreneur

Everything else can be done by someone else for very little money. You own your own business. You have pride in it and in your role running it. Almost certainly you're convinced there are things you do in your business that no one else can. I used to think that, too. It took me many years to get over the fact that anything I do, someone else can do, too—and usually better than I can. That's a hard pill for a testosterone-laden man to swallow. Most never do, and consequently, they die never knowing the freedom that comes with delegation.

I wish I'd had a book like this one when I started my real estate business in 1982. I had been a struggling auto mechanic/service station manager until then, swapping hours for dollars, living day to day with no money left over at the end of the week. I had already been married to my wife, Beverly, for seventeen years (it was fifty years on September 18, 2015). I had four kids, and my whole life was work. A twelve-hour day was a short one. I was convinced if I didn't put in the time I couldn't make a living, and of course, no mechanic could fix a car like me. I ran the shop, pumped gas, washed windows, did the books, and almost everything else myself, while neglecting the wife and four kids I left at home.

We were barely making ends meet, never had extra money, and bills were usually behind. There really wasn't an upside—no way to get rich or even raise our income. I was the boss but a slave to my business. It consumed me, and everything we did revolved around it. Forget vacations. I would have had to close to take one. If I'd been Beverly, I probably would have divorced me.

I knew I didn't want to do this forever, but I didn't have time to think about anything else. Then it happened . . .

A Washing Machine Changed Our Path Forever

I came home from work one night about half-past eleven, after closing the station, and Beverly told me the washing machine was broken. She wanted a new one.

I went into a rage over the fact we couldn't afford a new one, and my fit started a heated argument that lasted hours. I wanted to fix the old one, for the third time. She wanted a new one. There was about a $300 difference, and when you're buying groceries daily because you can't afford a week's worth, $300 is a fortune.

We both went to bed mad, and I lay there wide awake for hours. Then it hit me.

Ron, what a pathetic loser you are. Your wife of seventeen years, the mother of your four kids, asks you for a new washing machine to wash your filthy, greasy, stinking clothes, and you can't come up with a measly $300.

I kept asking myself, *What's wrong with me? Why are others doing so well, and I can't get ahead? How will this ever change?* I never got to sleep that night, but by the next morning, things felt different. I had to open the station at six, but for some reason I wasn't tired, and I went to work that day with a different attitude, actually looking forward to it for a change.

I didn't know what had happened then, but now I do. It's simple. Overnight, I made up my mind to find a way to create a better life for my family. I just snapped. "Enough of this shit," I said. "I'm better than this miserable existence, and I'm not going to take it anymore."

About three weeks later, after many hours of looking, I found my answer in an ad I noticed in the paper as I put it down for the dog to pee on. But before I get to that, I'll finish the washing machine story.

The next day I contacted a customer who owned an appliance store and cut a deal for a new washer. I gave him $50 in cash, and he agreed to take the rest out in gas. The cost of this brand-spanking-new Amana was $328. How I remember that, I don't know, but there was one condition on my end: he had to deliver the machine and set it up that day. This he did.

The ad was for a real estate seminar that taught people how to do deals with nothing down. It said I could buy and sell houses using no money or credit, and that appealed to me, since I had neither. I went to an evening seminar, which led me to a two-day seminar costing $450, money I had to borrow. Most of that seminar was like a foreign language to me, but I absorbed one technique that got me my first check in three weeks. The rest is history: more than three thousand houses bought and sold and still doing two to four a month, while spending less than five hours of my time on real estate. Thus, this book.

When I did my first real estate deal and got my first check for $3,000, I called my boss that day and told him, "I'm upping my income—up yours." I haven't been back since. I felt incredible pride as I embarked on a business buying and selling houses, but I had no idea what I was doing. I did not know how to delegate or automate. My entire staff was me, me, and me. I changed jobs without changing habits. Soon my real estate business became just as life sucking as the service station.

Two years into the business, I recruited my sixteen-year-old daughter, Vicki, to help me with administrative tasks and started assigning her things to do. To my amazement, she was actually able to complete these jobs without my input. That was an important small step, but the bulk of the business still weighed me down.

Then one day, three grueling years in, I decided to go on a weeklong vacation. I did this knowing full well that when I came back, my business would be destroyed. I'd have to start all over again because there was no way that a business could survive without me, the owner, being there for a whole week. Remember, there was no email or texting back then, no photos or documents sent instantly through cyberspace. We had landlines and direct mail, so there was really no way to communicate other than by telephone.

Did I enjoy myself on that vacation? Of course not. All I could think about was the mess I was going to have to clean up when I got back. Finally, I made it back, and lo and behold, not only had everything gone okay, but sales were actually up! I'm a man, so I figured that was a fluke and that it would never happen again.

The next year, I went on another vacation, and the same thing happened. Shocking, I know, but the world went on without me. Decisions were made because they had to be made. When my daughter had the ability and the authority to make those decisions and wasn't waiting on me, they got made quickly—and most of them were correct. Some weren't. Nobody died.

Over time, I learned to let loose. My next vacation was two weeks long. By then, I had three people on my payroll, including a secretary. I went away, and when I came back, incredibly, everything was fine. Gradually, I loosened the reins. It wasn't easy, I admit, but I started assigning more and more tasks to other people.

Another revelation came shortly after this, when a seller called wanting to sell me a house. I pretty much did the deal over the telephone. All I needed to do was go to the house and get the paperwork. Well, I was tied up and couldn't make it, so I said to my secretary, "This is the paperwork. Go to the house and get them to sign it here and here and here." Lo and behold, when I got back to the office, she had every "t" crossed and "i" dotted, even though she didn't necessarily understand the documents or know what they were signing.

Afterward, I heard her on the telephone with the seller, and they sounded buddy-buddy, like best friends. *Holy cow*, I thought to myself, *she did a better job of that than I would have.* I would have gotten the paperwork signed, but she actually made a friend of the seller. She was better at creating relationships than I was. Once I realized this, I started delegating more and more to her.

Over time, I learned if you surround yourself with good people, then they can do pretty much anything you can do—if you'll let them. Therein lies the key: will you let them? If you can learn to turn over tasks, if you can take the advice in this book, the payoff is enormous, not just in your business but in your personal life as well.

Not only did I enjoy my vacations once I learned to delegate, but I also began enjoying the time when I was off work because everything wasn't on my shoulders. Most tasks and responsibilities were on someone else's shoulders—I'd delegated them. Over the years, I developed what I think of as "greasy shoulders," meaning the monkey can't get on my back and hang on long. It's too slippery up there. It's slippery because I delegate projects as fast as I can, and then they become someone else's job. All I have to do is follow up and see that projects get completed, and even this sort of supervision can be delegated.

I still buy and sell two to four houses a month, but that job has become very part-time for me. I spend, at most, maybe five hours a month on it. Why? Today, we are automated, and virtual assistants do almost all the manual labor. Anything else, I delegate. The only decisions I make today in my housing business are what houses I want to buy and which buyers I want to sell to. The facts are collected and parties prescreened before I know either exists. Nearly everything else is handled by my personal assistant or virtual assistants or is outsourced.

My systems are taught worldwide. This book is a product of many years of doing it the hard way. I used that experience to set up systems for my clients to use, allowing them to bypass those years and eliminate many expensive lessons.

Don't think for a minute this is a real estate book. These lessons are the same regardless of your product or service, but because I've been teaching real estate since 1987, you also shouldn't be surprised when the subject comes up again.

By the way, I also own two restaurants, a multimillion-dollar publishing company that sells and delivers real estate training, a consulting company, a membership company, a virtual assistant service, a sales floor, multiple real estate ventures, and other assorted endeavors—none of which requires me to show up in the morning anymore.

Compare my approach with that of the deli owner whose shop I recently bought, and consider which model your business most resembles. The owner of the sandwich shop, which I bought for my twenty-four-year-old granddaughter Christy, ran it for one year. During that time, he was present every hour it was open. He ran the shop six days a week, without a break.

"Why are you selling?" I asked him.

"I'm just tired," he said. "I can't leave this place because it won't run without me."

Well, I bought it and put my granddaughter, who happened to have four or five years' experience running a Subway shop, in charge. Of course, she works there most of the time that it's open but not all of it. She has taken control of her own schedule by adding people at slow times when she doesn't really need to be there.

The previous owner could never do that because he just didn't have any systems in place. He didn't have any control—not of his time, his money, or his business. He worked from six in the morning until nine at night, six days a week—for nothing. He wasn't making any money. He was afraid people were going to steal from him and things couldn't survive without him, until the business ruined his life, and he had to get out.

Finally, he sold that sandwich shop for less money than he'd paid for it a year prior, which isn't uncommon in the restaurant industry, I might add. It's a classic case of a business running an owner, not an owner running a business.

The sandwich shop owner knew there were things he should be doing to make his business succeed, but he didn't have the time to focus on them. Because of his approach, he could barely leave the building. He knew that he should be doing catering and probably delivery, and he should get out and circulate to let the neighborhood know he was there. He didn't have time to do any of that. He was too busy making sandwiches to get people to buy them.

He should have focused on revenue, getting new business, growing the business. He chose to work for the $8 per hour his replacement would cost.

I discovered, when I do less, I really do make more because I can sit back and run my business from a thirty thousand-foot view. I can see the big picture and think like an owner, not an employee. I can focus on creating more revenue with less expenditure and less grief by automating, systemizing, and delegating.

That's fine for sandwiches or real estate, Ron, but that wouldn't work for my business.

Yes, it will, if you let it. It makes no difference what your product or service is. For instance, I talk to chiropractors, doctors, and dentists all the time because I teach them how to invest in real estate, and they all come to the same conclusion sooner or later: This practice is great as long as I'm here, but when I'm not here, my income stops. When I'm the only one producing income, I'm in a very dangerous situation.

They start to wonder what will happen when they don't want to do the same job anymore. What will happen if their retirement isn't what they'd hoped or when the government legislates them out of business? They start to feel trapped in their businesses, and this is when they come to me. Their mind-set is usually, "I'm the doctor. How is the business going to go on without me?"

I have actually had many doctor clients who come to me, learn real estate, and decide they don't want to work in medicine anymore because they're making more money in housing. However, most don't close their practices. They hire another doctor to staff the office. They might make less money from medicine, but they no longer have to devote their lives to it. Now, all they have to do is watch the operation from that thirty thousand-foot view, pull whatever money they can out of it, and make more money doing other things.

As a real estate trainer, I get people from all fields who come in and quickly learn this lesson. Real estate is so systemized and automated the way I do it and the way I teach it that it takes very little time from the owner. As I said, I spend fewer than five hours a month at it and do quite well. I'll discuss time management in chapter 5, and in chapter 10, "Real Estate Ron's Way," I'll go over exactly how I run this business in just five hours per month.

Perhaps you haven't yet reached the point where you're selling your business out of desperation, but be honest with yourself and think about the diagnostic test you took at the start of this chapter. Is your style of management more like the deli owner's (working twelve-hour days, overseeing minutiae, and making small or no profits, without time to see the big picture) or more like mine (working five hours a month, delegating most tasks, earning high profits, and focusing solely on revenue and decision making)? Which model makes more sense?

My goal in this book is to help you move from the life of pain experienced by that sandwich shop owner and countless other business owners to a life in which you are in control. This isn't nuclear physics. You don't need to be a genius to delegate, automate, and systematize in ways that allow you to make more by doing less. You only have to explore honestly the problems that are weighing you down and begin to take the steps, outlined in the following chapters, to take back your business and your life.

CHAPTER 2

Why Most Businesses Fail

Not Your Fault? Yes It Is!

More than half of small businesses close within their first five years, and two-thirds shut down within a decade. Why they fail is no mystery—the mistakes are easy to identify, and we'll explore them in this chapter.

Most business owners don't fail from a lack of intelligence or hard work. They tend to be smart, ambitious, hardworking, and passionate about something they do well. But being intelligent doesn't mean you're running your business intelligently. In my experience, business operators often suffer from shortsightedness. Their view of the business is from close-up and on the ground—not from the thirty thousand-foot height that allows them to see the big picture, to focus on decision making, and to prioritize revenue.

If your business isn't making as much money as you'd like, the odds are good that you aren't doing too little. You're doing too much, or too much of the wrong thing. While you're hard at work on minutiae, you're neglecting revenue creation and following a recipe which, if it doesn't lead to failure, certainly won't bring the kind of success you want.

Are you going to ride the road to failure and become another statistic, or are you going to do less to make more? Are you going to get out of your own way? If the test you took in chapter 1 indicated some of the pain and frustration you feel running your business day to day, then you're probably lacking in one or more of these key areas, the top reasons businesses fail. They are:

- weak marketing

- undercapitalization

- poorly conceived products

- lack of due diligence

- big ego

- poor time management

Now let's go through these categories and highlight the ways business owners fail in each. Solving these problems will require systemizing, delegating, and automating, so you can get out of your own way and focus on revenue creation.

Weak Marketing

One of my pet peeves in my travels talking to business owners of all kinds, especially operators of brick-and-mortar businesses, is their lack of marketing know-how. I am appalled at the ignorance owners have when it comes to attracting customers. Incredibly, people seem to believe that if you open it, they will come. There is no evidence to support this idea.

What happens if you open it and they don't come? Any smart business owner should have a marketing plan to attract customers before he or she ever even thinks about opening the door. All businesses have products and services. Regardless of your business, the first step of a successful plan is to find people who are interested in those products and services. How are you locating prospects?

In my real estate business, this task is done for me by virtual assistants (VAs). VAs locate the properties for sale by owner (FSBOs) online and call them to fill out a property info sheet. With today's technology, locating prospects is not that difficult, regardless of what product or service you sell, but if you don't create a consistent system for finding prospects, then you're waiting for people to come to your door instead of forcing them through it.

In my restaurant business, I hire a media company to handle all of my social media, to post videos and special offers. We also distribute coupons through magazines such as *Mint* and other publications distributed nearby. I am not interested in attracting people who live across town because if I get them to the restaurant, they probably won't come back. I'm only interested in drawing people I can turn into regular customers, so my marketing circle has a radius of five miles from the restaurant. This seems obvious to me, but it's not obvious to most.

We give away discount coupons to attract business and—this is important—I measure their effectiveness. I know the numbers. Every time a $10 coupon is redeemed, I track its gross revenue. The ones that are working, we might continue, and the ones that aren't, we stop using. In a nutshell, I don't just assume people will walk in.

I force them to walk in by appealing to their greed glands and giving them free food.

In my publishing business, Global Publishing, Inc., we spend approximately $50,000 a month running radio ads and buying traffic online and through direct mail to drive folks into a free offer of my book and CD. It costs me about $100 for every one of those customers I get who gives me a small amount of money. I would be an idiot if I didn't know what that customer is worth and how long it takes to get that money back.

If your outgo exceeds your income, your upkeep will be your downfall.

For Global, it takes about ninety days to recapture our loss.

However, I also know that over the first year, we have a substantial gain and actually profit because we're willing to take that loss on the front-end. How many businesses do you know where acquiring customers is free? A business that is not willing to spend a little money to acquire a customer and create a lifetime of value is a business that truly doesn't understand marketing. In chapter 6, we'll focus on marketing in greater detail, exploring how to create and measure a marketing campaign that's effective for your business.

Undercapitalization

Many business owners grossly underestimate the amount of capital required to get their business up and running. Sometimes they simply look at the cost of acquiring the business, stocking the business, and three months of operating expenses. I don't know about you, but Murphy lives here. With everything I do, Murphy's camped out right next door to wreak havoc and destroy all those beautiful spreadsheets created before we opened the business.

I recently bought a seafood restaurant. My purchase price to date is approximately 40 percent of the total capital required to get this business up and running and to give it the best chance of success. Fortunately, I had enough experience to know this before I made the investment, but what if I hadn't? What if this was the first restaurant I bought, and I didn't have the capital? The answer is simple: I would be out of business, and that is exactly why you see many restaurants open and close in a matter of months.

FYI: my first break-even month was five months after the purchase, and the restaurant was operating when I bought it.

Make sure you know what your capital needs are before you open or expand any business. If that capital is not available, put on the brakes until it is, or switch to something else that falls within your capital constraints.

Poorly Conceived Products

Inexperienced business owners often think because they have something to sell somebody will buy it. They don't believe the quality of that product or service is a critically important factor. It is.

You can't make chicken salad out of chicken shit.

Selling something is one thing, but keeping it sold is another. If the product is not quality, the consumer has every right to return it. If the service is of poor quality, the consumer will not come back.

The old saying is, "For every customer you upset, there are fifteen more you'll never hear from." It's a lot easier to piss off people than it is to gain their confidence. If you deliver crap, then your business will soon become crap, and you'll be looking for something else to do. Take a good hard look at what you're selling. Is your ego getting in the way of reality? What have you done to determine the real value of that product or service to the consumer who wants to buy it?

Does your product or service make a difference in their lives? Do they brag about it to other people? Is it something they would buy again? Are you proud to talk about it? Are you proud to sell it? Will you stand behind it? If not, you should address this problem before you even think about the business start-up or operations. Start with what you can deliver that will sustain a long-lasting business.

I'm in the real estate training industry. I teach people how to buy and sell houses. I've been doing that for twenty-nine years. I have competition. I've seen a lot of companies come and go because they deliver crap. We are here for the long run because our product and services are quality. What we teach works, and over the years, we have collected mountains of evidence to prove it throughout North America and beyond.

It's a whole lot easier to sell stuff than to deliver stuff. Many companies implode because they get good at selling but not very good at delivering. I've seen a lot of them come and go. In fact, I can honestly say, I have the longest tenure of any company still teaching real estate because we know the sale is only the beginning. Now we have to deliver what we sell . . . darn it.

At least half our staff is dedicated to serving and not to sales or marketing. While my competitors, mostly my students, were taking all the money for themselves over the years, I put most of our income back into the business's infrastructure so we'd be here thirty years later.

Lack of Due Diligence

Too many business owners fail to do their homework and, instead, proceed with blinders on. They plunge in without really understanding what happens behind the scenes. You cannot learn how to run a restaurant by eating in restaurants. Being a customer doesn't teach you the things you must learn to be an owner.

Is there a market for your product or service? I advise all my clients to see if there's a market for what they want to sell before spending the time and energy to make it. I've created real estate courses many times in the past only to find out there was no interest in them. They take up space on the shelf, but they don't produce much revenue. I learned over the years to check the market first and then move into the creation and implementation.

I closed a restaurant a few years ago because I hadn't done any research on the concept and opened up only to find out it was wrong for the location. Sadly, I didn't figure that out before taking a million-dollar seminar at Hard Knocks University. Gosh, these lessons are expensive.

I sold that restaurant to a group that did have the right concept, and they're doing very well . . . at my expense. Glad I got that off my chest. I feel better now.

Before I open a business today, if possible, I hire a company to do a feasibility study. There have been many ventures that I intended to pursue until a feasibility study came back and told me what a dumb idea it was.

Once, I planned to put windmills on a piece of property I had in Michigan. I commissioned a feasibility study, which told me that the location would be a good place for windmills—except that there was no wind. This news killed that project pretty quickly.

Another time, I was going to do a housing development in Georgia. We did a feasibility study to determine whether there was a market for the houses we were going to build. We realized when the study came back that, gosh, no one had pulled a building permit in that city in two years. Too many business owners bring a thing to market, and then it turns out there isn't any market. Check the market first!

Getting the lay of the land requires help. You cannot collect all the necessary facts on your own, no matter how good you are on the Internet. Let professionals who know where to dig surface all of the negative and positive facts regarding a business before you decide it's time to plunge in. I say this knowing full well most business owners don't want this expense. Instead of spending a little bit of money getting a feasibility study done, they'll spend a fortune figuring out they're heading down the wrong path. A good feasibility study will predict business results based on pertinent factors and the results similar companies have already seen. A feasibility study is not an unnecessary expense but is the cheapest insurance you can buy.

A feasibility study will assess the need for your product or service, but you should also honestly assess your own level of experience. If you're opening a business in which you're not experienced, it might be a smart idea to go to work for someone else already in that field to learn the ropes. Learn at their expense, not yours.

Big Ego

Only you can do it?

Wrong.

As discussed previously, owners who try to do everything themselves are limiting their potential. If you and only you can do it, great, but the list of such tasks should be extremely short—and getting shorter all the time. If it's not, trust me, you're headed toward extinction. However long that list of essential tasks is, my goal in this book is to help you find ways to make it even shorter.

Some of this will be accomplished by changing your processes and habits, which we'll discuss in the next two chapters. The chapters on delegating, outsourcing, and time management also will shorten that list.

If you have a healthy ego, and as a business owner, it's likely you do, it isn't easy to delegate, but you should be working daily to shorten the list of things you personally have to handle. There is really nothing in your business you can't get someone else to do, and we'll discuss this in detail in later chapters.

Poor Time Management

People are always asking me how I get so much done. They think I have the memory of an elephant when, in fact, the opposite is true. I have no memory. I age quickly. As I write this book, I'm almost seventy years old. If I had to rely on my memory, I'd be an unorganized mess like most people in our society.

I have a very simple system. It's called a time planner. This system allows me to write down not only the things I need to do every day but also my ideas. It forces me to put in print what goes through my mind, so I don't lose great ideas, and I time-activate everything that needs to be done, which includes keeping my promises. When I make a promise, I write it down in my planner, so I don't have to remember that I made it. I put it under the date when I intend to keep it, and when I open up my planner on that day, it will be right there. I can set it and forget it.

When others make promises to me, I note them in my planner, too, and they are shocked to learn that I actually remember their promises several days or weeks later, when those pledges haven't been fulfilled. They think I have an incredible memory, but I just write things down. This is a habit you must acquire if you're ever going to get organized. Unless you start writing things down, the greatest ideas in the world become farts in the wind. They never get acted on.

You'll never see me without a pen and something to write on. I can't tell you how many big decisions I've made or big ideas I've had sitting in restaurants and writing them down on napkins, some for multimillion-dollar projects. If I don't write something down, I use a recorder.

With a cell phone, the recorder is right there with you everywhere you go, so it's very easy to record these ideas so you don't lose them. There's really no excuse for not writing down or capturing electronically the things that you must do and can't afford to forget.

I can forecast out one, two, or three years in advance because I write everything down, and then when the time comes to take action, the task is before me, and I either take it or pass on it because it's no longer worth taking action on. I'll cover in detail the many ways I use my own planner in chapter 5.

Business is full of minutiae, endless small things that have to be done day-in and day-out. If these things aren't written down and checklists created, then minutiae will suck up all of your productive time. Spending half your day thinking about what you should do because you don't have a checklist is not effective and can result in paralysis. A little bit of movement is better than a boatload of meditation.

The main message of this book is the less I do, the more I make. This involves systemizing, delegating, and automating, but you can't do any of these unless you get in the habit of writing things down, so you don't forget them. This is the only way to get the important things done.

The bottom line?

If you're going to succeed in business, you must get shit done.

CHAPTER 3

You're Not That Special

Can Your Business Run without You?

I previously mentioned how when I started in real estate back in 1982, I thought my business wouldn't run without me. It took a long time to figure out this just wasn't the case. After years of training people in all walks of life, from professionals to the unemployed, I've recognized this same trait in many. I've met a lot of entrepreneurs who are under the impression that nothing can happen unless they're personally involved. The belief is especially strong in males of the species, who are overladen with testosterone. However, ladies, you have it, too. I've met an awful lot of women who seem to have more testosterone than some men.

You don't have to be personally involved in every chore and decision, and the sooner you realize this, the sooner you can get out of your own way. No business is going to provide you with the financial freedom you want unless it can run without you. And even more important for many business owners—they can't sell businesses that require their owners to run.

People are reluctant to buy businesses if the owners are so critical things won't work without them. It's a hard thing—to get out of the way—and the fix won't happen overnight, but there is no business which can't be systemized and automated to the point that it operates day to day largely without the owner's input.

I get dentists and doctors and all sorts of professionals coming to me and looking for a way to get out of their professions because the government is doing everything it can to put them out of business. Even more important, they wake up one day and realize the minute their hands quit working, their incomes quit flowing. It's a precarious position, knowing if you're down, your income stops.

That's one reason I like real estate so well. We not only make money in it almost immediately—measured in five- and six-figure checks—but we also can build residual income which doesn't depend on our participation. This income can last years—you do the job once and continually get paid for it.

In the medical and dental fields, doctors go to school for years, spend an awful lot of money on their education, and basically box themselves into a trap. The trap is that they've got so much invested, they can't see themselves getting out. I can tell you from experience, after talking to many doctors and dentists, they would love to have an exit strategy before it's time to die. The problem is they don't know how the business can continue without them, so the general assumption is, "I'm stuck here whether I like it or not."

Some smart doctors I've talked to have figured it out. The answer is simple: systemize the business with policies and procedures. Develop a plan in which everything that needs to happen in the building is written down and, as much as possible, put things on autopilot. Then replace yourself with another doctor who can do any job you can do for some rather small amount of money. I've seen so many professionals do this, and they wind up working one or two days a week. It excites me to see they actually can take their lives back and escape the traps their businesses have become.

In my business of buying and selling houses, I do one thing—make decisions. When we buy houses, generally, they are beautiful homes in beautiful neighborhoods, and we buy them on terms. "Terms" means we buy them with a lease purchase or with owner financing.

In today's market, about one-third of owners with homes listed "for sale by owner," or FSBO, will consider terms if asked properly. We have a property information sheet our virtual assistants fill out to collect all the data. Literally, these are the questions they ask: "Would you consider selling on a lease purchase and/or would you consider taking your equity in monthly installments?" When the answers come back "yes," these FSBOs turn into prospects.

The virtual assistants call the prospects, not me, not even my staff. Virtual assistants are not on the payroll. They are paid by the minute, for actual work done, not by the hour for sitting in the building. We have created our own entire floor of virtual assistants to service our students around the country, and they make twenty-five thousand calls to FSBOs every month and fill out property information sheets for them and ask the questions concerning the terms.

In my personal business, I use the exact same VAs my students do. One of their jobs is to go online and actually find for-sale-by-owner ads on various websites, call those folks, and fill out the forms. My virtual assistants create leads for our students this way, and the students don't even know it's going on. The VAs just call them up and send the leads to the students.

Here is the extent of my participation on my own deals. I simply scan the sheets, looking at the numbers and the answers the sellers have given, and assess which ones are worth following up with a phone call from a member of my staff, who will read a script I've created to determine if the property is worth visiting. VAs call the leads. I have one person making the final call and making the appointment, and then I have another person going to the house and getting a contract signed, if warranted, or leaving one and allowing the seller a day or two to take it to an attorney or go over it themselves.

In the entire process of buying houses, my only role is deciding which sellers are worth pursuing. I turn down a lot of deals most people would be happy to have because I focus on quality, not quantity. In fact, if a real estate transaction today doesn't have a net profit of at least $20,000, it's just not worth my time. And to be honest, that one doesn't excite me a whole lot either.

On the selling side, the entire process is also automated. My virtual assistants put ads on the web, and I have a local virtual assistant who puts up signs pointing to the houses. Those two things alone generate calls from potential buyers, who are directed into an Interactive Voice Response system (IVR). This system is set up to take calls from buyers twenty-four hours a day, with no human interference. It automatically asks the questions and gets the answers we need, things such as: "How much do you have to put down? How much can you pay per month? How many bedrooms do you want? What part of town do you want to live in?"

Since we sell on terms, the amount the customer has to put down is our main concern. Our buyers cannot qualify for a loan today, for whatever reason, whether it's credit or debt ratio or some other problem. About 80 percent of people looking to buy a house can't qualify for a loan, so when I offer them terms—a lease purchase or seller financing—I'm ten times more likely to sell that house than the Realtors who are looking for all-cash buyers who qualify at the bank.

I can sell much faster and easier, at a higher price, and never would I put a tenant-buyer in a house without collecting a nonrefundable option deposit in the thousands. By offering terms, we get a higher price and several thousand dollars upfront, and we lease-option the property to the buyers until they can qualify.

The immediate income comes from that down payment deposit, which ranges from $10,000 to $100,000, depending on the price range of the house. We're in and out in thirty to sixty days max, with no costly entitlements. There are no rehabs, loans, short sales, or Realtors—none of the things people think have to be involved in real estate. My entire involvement in the sales process is deciding which buyers I will accept. And I can tell you, the decision is easy if they have a lot of money to put down.

In fact, the amount of money they put down will be in front of me before we ever contact them. Then one of my virtual assistants will call them and fill out a form using my script. The assistant will also set a meeting but only if I'm satisfied a buyer can meet my requirements for both the down payment and a monthly payment. At that point, my decision is, do I want them or not? From then on, the attorney does everything. The attorney closes the transaction and prepares the documents. The only work I've done is deciding which seller and buyer I want.

For years, I've been making millionaires all over North America by teaching my students the same systems and helping them to get out of their own way. It doesn't take long to teach people real estate. Getting them systemized and automated, helping them learn how to actually run a business, is a tougher, longer process, especially if they've come from the job market and have been someone else's employee all their lives.

We spend more time getting people to do the right things than we do teaching them real estate. We have mentors who work with them as they go through the deals, literally forcing them to get checks and stay on track and stay systemized. It sometimes amazes even me how little it takes to get people off track, even after intense training.

Even with somebody standing beside them, beating them with a bloody stick, they still want to do the kinds of labor-intensive grunt work they've been doing their entire lives. But, ultimately, we get most of them to come around. The endgame usually occurs about a year in. By then, they are running their own businesses the way I run mine and freeing themselves up to do the things in life they never had the time or money to do before.

Most people who get into the real estate business, buying and selling houses, fall into the same minutia-laden trap. They spend all their time doing worthless, needless tasks that do nothing but waste time. I spend less than five hours a week in my real estate business, and some of my top students, netting more than a million dollars a year, spend less time than that. You'll see some examples of those folks in this book, people like Jay Connor, Tom and Cindy Dumire, Brian and Lynette Wolff, and many more.

Right now, I imagine, some business owners who are drowning in minutia are saying to themselves, that's fine for real estate, but I could never get my business on autopilot.

Yes, you can! I have done just that with multiple businesses in a variety of fields over many years. Let's look at a couple examples.

I have a restaurant in Jacksonville, Florida, called Iggy's Seafood Shack. I bought an operating restaurant, changed the menu, and brought in some new staff. I didn't really touch the interior, which is a lesson I learned from my last restaurant. There, I built out and lost a lot of money because the concept didn't work. It's a mistake I won't make again. Any restaurant I buy in the future will already be built out at someone else's expense.

At Iggy's, we operated under the old flag for about a month, until we were able to put the new menu in place. What is my level of participation in this restaurant? Around 90 percent of my real estate business is done by virtual assistants, but obviously, you can't run a restaurant with VAs. How can you stay out of your own way in this sort of business?

Well, let me start by saying, the day I have to put on an apron and actually work at Iggy's will be the day I get out of the restaurant business. The first thing I did was find a general manager who'd worked for me before, who I trusted, and told him to go find us a restaurant. Once we found and purchased the place, my job was to automate the processes as much as possible. I helped get the menu in order, but I can't say I created it. I just gave my input, mostly by indicating what I like to eat. I mean, why else own a restaurant? (Incidentally, I've never stood in line to eat there, and pretty much everything on the menu is something I like).

Over three months or so, the general manager fixed one problem after another until we finally got the restaurant to the point to where it runs rather well, the income is rising sharply, and it is making a profit. I can't say this was the case when I bought it. When you achieve breakeven status in a restaurant, you've pretty much hit a triple. From there, it becomes easy to constantly focus on the systems and drive the revenue up, especially if you know anything about marketing.

My point is, the extent of my input was to help the staff design the systems and also, for a while, to run the marketing program, which was largely coupon related. Through marketing, which I'll cover in depth in chapter 6, I drove the revenue up quickly and acquired a lot of new customers. I don't wash dishes. I don't cook. I don't wait tables. I don't sweep floors. In fact, I only go there to eat.

I'm gradually getting out of my role in marketing Iggy's, too, but I'll never be totally out of the restaurant—I don't want to be. My job in any company I own is to drive revenue. I'm the owner. If I don't drive the revenue, no one else will. The general manager of a restaurant can't focus on revenue when he or she is focused on delivering food in a timely and consistent manner, handling issues and complaints, and the like. And it's hard—almost impossible, actually—for business owners to stay focused on revenue when they're being sucked into the minutia.

At Iggy's, I'm not that special, and sorry if this hurts your ego, but at your business, neither are you. You can and must realize this if you're going to get out of your own way.

My publishing company, Global Publishing, Inc., is an even better example of how any owner can put any business on autopilot. At first glance, I would appear to have an irreplaceable role at Global. This is the company I started to help people invest in real estate and generate income. It sells and delivers all of my seminars and publishes all of the products I create, including my DVDs and CDs. Global markets the systems that generate leads, convert them to customers, and then service the customers.

I actually have three functions at this company. The first is to write sales copy. The second is to speak and teach, and the third is to create chaos and drive revenue. I make almost no decisions. They're made by our COO, Jennifer Shedlin, and her executive staff. Global Publishing has about sixty employees, but I never show up for work before noon. Half the time, no one even knows when I'm there (and I'm guessing they would just as soon I stayed home).

One of the functions I perform for Global is to stand on the stage once or twice a month and teach. I'm the guru. Most people would think this position couldn't be filled by someone else, but even as the guru, the Colonel Sanders of Global, I can be replaced. For a period of about five years, I never went out and taught any of our four-day trainings. I had a very qualified person doing that for me. Only when the recession hit in 2008 did I decide to go back and do it myself. I have been doing it ever since and will continue to as long as I enjoy it. The minute I don't, I'll replace myself.

I write copy at the company because I still want to and because I can. I'm a pretty good copywriter, but this is a job that can easily be filled by another qualified copywriter. There is nothing I do in any of my businesses—even Global—which someone else can't do if I'm not around.

The most important thing I do at Global is drive revenue by creating chaos. I won't let my staff stand still or get lackadaisical. I'm constantly pushing them and coming up with new things to drive revenue—events, marketing plans, ideas for lead generation. My COO is conservative, so I have to be the revenue driver.

I also run three consulting businesses, "mastermind groups," where people pay me a substantial amount of money for three meetings per year. Some might think those companies can't run without me, but even there, I have replaced myself with quality leaders to head the mastermind groups many times, and it has worked quite nicely.

I have started and run many successful businesses around the idea that I'm not that special, and I hope by now you are starting to realize that you aren't either. You are not vital to the day to day operations at your business. In fact, it's vital to your business that you get out of the day to day operations and stop wallowing in minutia. Getting out of your own way starts with accepting this idea, but putting it into practice is not easy. To do that, you'll have to work at changing your habits, which is the focus of our next chapter.

CHAPTER 4

Changing Habits

Are You Willing to Change?

In this chapter, we'll tackle what might be the most difficult task of them all—actually changing your habits. It takes many years to acquire habits. Are you willing to take a few months to change them?

If not, nothing will alter.

Read all the books you want, listen to all the CDs you can find, and immerse yourself in the most positive affirmations out there. Make lists and design spreadsheets and charts until you're half blind—all of that's worthless unless you make the conscious decision you're going to do things differently than you've been doing them.

Bill Wallace said, "Your biggest challenge will be getting out from under the never-ending wave of bullshit long enough to do anything profitable—even one thing a day." He's right.

Altering habits is difficult but mandatory if permanent change is the goal.

Most people in business need to work on changing a handful of common bad habits in order to take control of their time and their thought process. In the next chapter, I'll deal with time management Ron's way and talk about my strategies for remembering things— or, more accurately, for never having to remember them—as well as for keeping promises and holding others accountable for theirs. Setting aside a larger time management strategy for now, I'd like to focus on five key, closely related areas where most business owners must change their habits if they want to get ahead. These are positive, practical steps you can start taking tomorrow—or better yet, *right now,* to achieve quick results by freeing up time! The most common bad habits in business arise in these areas:

- managing information flow

- managing calls and emails

- resisting the urge to do it yourself

- limiting your accessibility

- thinking big

Now let's take a look at each of these areas, which might seem small but, in fact, eat up hours like a deceptively skinny champion downing hot dogs at a competitive eating contest.

Managing Information Flow

Are you consuming valuable, pertinent information, or is junk information consuming you? In this day of constant information flow from endless sources, it's not hard to see why solicitations and requests from the people around you—both business and personal associates—consume so much time. If you're not careful, incoming info can consume most of your day. Perhaps it already does, without your even realizing it.

The first conscious step in changing the bad habits you've developed around information flow is to delegate it. In my case, this job falls to my personal assistant, Tish Hill, who regulates the flow for me and drains off most information before it ever has a chance to reach my desk.

Yes, I have email and I get emails and texts just like everyone else, but I'm very selective about who gets my email address, which in itself cuts down on a lot of my personal email traffic. Most of those calling and emailing you want something. You have to be tough—realize they don't have your best interests at heart, and screen them out accordingly.

Business is no place for weaklings who think everyone does what they say and gives a rat's ass whether they succeed or die. Others would rather you fail. It gives them strength and something to gossip about. They'll take advantage of your weaknesses, amplify your mistakes, and scheme behind your back.

Nonetheless, when I get to the office on the days I work, there's always paper in my basket and business emails that my personal assistant has determined need my attention. There's always somebody wanting something, whether it's from outside my business or my own staff. I have a very simple system to handle paper as it comes in.

I FART on it.

Before you think I've gone off the deep end with a vulgar comment, let me explain. FART stands for the four options you have for paperwork—File, Act, Reroute, or Trash—and it indicates the attitude you should take toward most paper, which does nothing but waste time. Let's look at my personal system. As I'm sitting behind my desk, to my left are two trays. One is for incoming papers, and one is for outgoing papers. When I get to work, there's always a pile of papers in the incoming tray. My goal is to dispose of that paperwork as quickly as possible and thereby dispose of all tasks related to it, so I can get on to the things that I've scheduled for the day.

First let's look at how paper gets into the inbox because let me assure you, most candidates for that receptacle don't make it past my office door. My personal assistant looks at everything that comes through, both paper and electronic mail, and determines whether it'll even need my attention. If it does, she prints it and puts it in the pile for me (she only forwards email to me electronically if it's important enough that I need to see it right away—most emails that aren't deleted get printed and put on the pile).

This process alone eliminates probably three-quarters of the paperwork that I would handle if she weren't managing it for me. Having a good gatekeeper also means I don't even see more than three-quarters of the emails from people I have no reason to respond to. Many of them have sent emails unsolicited, and all of them seem to want something. If you're human and operate in the world of business, I'm sure you get these sorts of emails and solicitations, too, and you probably don't want to see them any more than I do.

Once Tish has assembled a pile of paperwork and put it in front of me, one of four things will happen to every item in that pile: I will File it, Act on it, Reroute it, or Trash it . . . FART on it.

For me, to "File" a paper simply means I put it in the out-basket and write the word "File" on it. My personal assistant either files it then or has someone else file it. Caution: be careful what you file. If you put everything you receive on paper into a filing cabinet, pretty soon you'll need four filing cabinets, and the reality is, 90 percent of their contents is better suited for the trash can. If you feel you couldn't face a major problem without a particular piece of paper being available, put it in the file. If that's not the case, put it in the trash can.

The papers I will "Act" on are items needing further attention. The required action might be to write a note or letter, or to take some physical action. If the paper requires action on my part, I put it in a pile that I spread vertically on my desk in front of me with the intention of acting on it as soon as I've processed the pile. I try not to leave until the pile has been processed, so my desk is clean.

The third option is to "Reroute" a piece of paperwork. To reroute it, all I do is jot the name of the staff member, virtual assistant, or personal assistant who I want to take care of it and then drop it in the outbox. Sometimes I scribble instructions on it, but often, even this isn't required.

Finally, we come to my favorite option: "Trash" it. This is where probably 90 percent of my incoming paperwork winds up, in the trash. Most of it is just stuff I need to read, and once I have, it's disposed of. Again, be careful not to keep paperwork that really has no significance. My trash can is a favorite destination for paperwork on my desk.

Again, my goal is to leave a clean desk behind me every single day. It bothers me to leave junk on my desk to be dealt with later. If you can't figure out what to do with it, trash it. The world will not end. You will likely never need it again.

This simple system has served me well for a lot of years. It can serve you, too, keeping the clutter out of your way and what you need in front of you. Even more important, it will improve your mind-set. A cluttered working area reflects a cluttered mind. Clutter kills focus because you feel overwhelmed and never know what to do next.

Managing Calls and Emails

The second haven for bad habits is in managing calls and emails. I described how I handle most emails above, but I have another stream of emails flowing to me through my iPad, too. We all have junk files, and mine is just as loaded as yours, but I don't even open my junk mail folder. Managing the other emails that fill my inbox each day is pretty simple because so few people have my email address. I'm so selective about who I give it to, I likely don't get more than forty or fifty emails a day. If those don't require action, most get instantly deleted.

I devote very little time to handling email. Yes, we all have breaks we can take to catch up on our emails, but don't let them control your life. My dinger is turned off, so I don't know when I get an email. I don't want to know because I won't allow incoming emails to interrupt my thought process or a task I'm trying to accomplish.

The same is true for my text dinger. If you read a text every time your phone dings—and these days, plenty of people do—consider how long it takes you to get back into the thought process interrupted by that text, likely a message with no value for you sent by someone with no legitimate reason to text you.

What if your new voicemail message was this: I'm sorry I missed your call, but I'm making some changes in life. If I don't return your call, you're one of them.

If you're going to control your time, you must immediately control your incoming calls, emails, and texts. I know it's a major undertaking to turn off the dingers that seem to structure our lives, but changing this one bad habit could add an hour or more to your day, and it's an important step in taking control of your time.

When I'm teaching a seminar, I absolutely insist that all phones be put away—no vibrating, dinging, or flashing—completely off and out of sight. I also alert my students that if they're looking down, I know exactly what they're doing. They're reading incoming texts or emails, and it's not allowed. When people pay me money to hear what I have to say, I demand enough attention to get my message out. After that, they can do with the information as they see fit. To me, looking at texts, reading emails, and even looking at a cell phone during a meeting is downright rude, and it won't happen in any meeting I'm conducting.

Resisting the Urge to Do It Yourself

The third habit to change is the urge to do it, whatever it is, yourself. This is going to be a big and very difficult habit for you to break if you're like most folks. Most of us, especially in business, think we have to have our hands in every little thing going on because it can't get done without us. We've discussed why this notion is false in previous chapters, and we'll continue to discuss it in future ones because it is the heart of this book. Unless you can train yourself to not do every little thing, this book can't help you. Nothing can help you if you don't work at changing this egotistical practice, the mother of all bad business habits.

Virtual assistants are easy to find and can do most of the things you currently do. Personal assistants are a choice I strongly recommend, and I'll explore why they're vital in chapter 7. I would never be without a personal assistant (PA) because they take a tremendous load off my back and manage my affairs without my presence. Yes, this is a full-time employee, but all the time you'll free up to focus on making decisions and driving revenue in your business should quickly justify the expense. The revenue increase needed to pay for a personal assistant is small, but the lifestyle change is huge when a PA takes over the grunt work, giving you the time to work on your business and not in it.

Every single time you sit down to do a task, ask yourself, "Is this the best use of my time?" Almost always, the answer will be no. Create a little sign for your desk asking this key question if this helps, or take a picture of the cover of this book, *The Less I Do, the More I Make*. Or write out in bold letters, WWRD: "What Would Ron Do?" Many of my students do exactly that and cure themselves of the worst of bad business habits: trying to do every little thing. Changing this habit takes time, but I can promise you, it's worth the effort.

Limiting Your Accessibility

No law requires you to be available every time someone wants your attention. You own your time. You're not obligated to other people, and they don't have the right to use your time unless you grant it to them. When you make yourself constantly accessible, you're at the mercy of others. Your time is their time—it's no longer yours—and, of course, in that case, most of it will get wasted. Do you take calls from folks when you don't know what the calls are about and there's no reason for you to believe they're in your best interest? Do you agree to meet folks simply because they ask, with no real purpose? Do you respond to texts and emails simply because you get them?

Let me repeat, you will not go to jail for ignoring requests to waste your time. If you train people to think they can interrupt you at will, then that's what they'll do. If you train them to know they can't interrupt you at will, then they won't. If you do not accept calls just because the phone rings, pretty soon, people understand you're not going to answer it, and in my experience, they quit calling, which is the whole point.

Of course, you'll take the calls, texts, and emails relevant to your business or to your personal life. But try an experiment. Track all of your communications on any random day, noting the time spent on each. You will be flabbergasted to see how few of those texts, calls, emails, and meetings matter. Now, think to yourself, what if I eliminate all of those time wasters? What if I put the world on notice and tell it, "I'm not your slave?" What if I return calls at my discretion? What if I return emails when I feel like it? What if I text back only when the mood strikes me or when it's necessary?

Yes, I know, this requires a major change of habits for most people. I get it. But I can tell you, once you establish the reputation that you're not openly accessible, most people gradually get the message: if they want to reach you, they have to go through proper channels. For me, that channel is my personal assistant or virtual assistant. You'll have to decide how easy you want to make it for people to get through to you. I get almost no calls from my hundreds of thousands of students, yet I'm listed in the phone book. I get almost no emails from them, and I get no texts from them, unless I'm working on a joint venture deal of some sort. All of that comes through my personal assistant before it has a chance to get to me.

Incidentally, my personal assistant is at the office. Yours doesn't have to be. Your personal assistant can be anywhere in the country with today's technology and be just as accessible as if he or she was ten feet away. I spend so much time out of the office, the truth is, almost all of my communications with my PA are remote and not face to face anyway. Recently, I was gone five days in a row, and my PA and I had only a few communications during that whole time.

That was all we needed to get everything done. And I could make a pretty long list of what got accomplished during this absence.

Thinking Big

The last habit to cultivate is the habit of thinking bigger. If you are the owner, the entrepreneur, or the boss, then you must decide what you're worth. If you think small, your business will remain small. If you set your standards and income goals low, that's where they'll stay. Set your standards higher. Create a revenue goal that scares you a little, and you might trick yourself into actually making it.

Do you want to earn a million dollars a year, or do you want to make half a million dollars a year? If you set your goal at half a million and achieve it, is that as good as setting it at a million and only getting half way there? Why not set the bar higher? Why can't you make more? What's stopping you? Don't underestimate the importance of attitude.

I deal with the same issues, live in the same world, and have to face the same gremlins that you and every other entrepreneur faces, day in and day out. I'll survive and fight like hell until I've won or died. I won't quit and no S.O.B. can or will take from me the one thing you can't buy—attitude. If it's positive, everything is easier. If it's negative, nothing is easy.

Start by making a list. In my planner I have a page called "Things I can do to create revenue." Most of those things are checked off, and I'm constantly adding new ones. If, in fact, your whole life isn't focused on minutia, running your business day in and day out to make a meager living, then you'll actually have time to think up ways of creating more revenue. Make a list and systematically work on it, trying the ideas that make sense and eliminating over time the ones that are not going to work or which don't fit into your lifestyle or plan.

Ted Turner said the biggest mistake he ever made was not setting his goals high enough. I find this to be true in most folks' lives. They just don't think they're worthy of making a lot more money. When people come to me to learn how to buy and sell houses, they come for the same reason. It revolves around money and financial freedom and retirement.

First, I have to train them in real estate, but I spend more time training them on how to run the business behind the real estate and in raising their expectations. The biggest problem for many is that they just don't feel worthy of making a lot of money. They haven't up to this point in their lives—they've been trained to be broke. We can just as easily get trained to be rich (by the way, rich is better).

To get rich, you must first take control of your time and get the grunt work off of your back. You'll get there a lot faster when you're focused on making decisions and driving revenue. You'll likely never get there if you don't find the will to change bad habits and start taking your life back on a daily basis. Many of the habit changes I've recommended are small, but together, they create large results.

Changing the habits we explored above is life changing, but time management is also a critical ingredient for growing your business and taking control of your life—so critical, we'll devote the entire next chapter to it.

CHAPTER 5

Manage Your Time

Time Is Money—How Do You Spend Yours?

I teach students at least two or three times a month in some city somewhere in America. When the discussion of getting things done comes up, the complaint always comes back to, "I just don't have time, Ron." My answer is always the same: "You have the same amount of time as Donald Trump, Bill Gates, Warren Buffet, me, and everyone else you know." The question is not whether or not you have time—it's whether you are willing to devote the time to do what you have to do in order to accomplish your goals.

Being busy will not make you rich. In fact, it can have the opposite effect and prevent you from ever achieving wealth. Don't get me wrong; rich people are busy, too. I'm very busy most of the time. There's always something chasing my attention and an endless supply of things to work on that suck up my time. The difference is that I constantly and consciously work on only those items I can't delegate and are worthy of my attention. Everybody is busy. Everybody has more to do than they really can get done. One has to make choices. If, in fact, your day is so loaded with minutia that you can't make time to get the important things done, well, this is the reason I wrote this book. Something must give. Only you can decide what it will be.

I might suggest you start by asking yourself, "Is this task I'm about to do going to accomplish anything of value? Is it going to make me any money? Is it going to benefit me or my family in any way? Is it going to increase the size or the volume of my business?" If the answer is no to all those questions, then obviously, it should be removed from the list to make room for something of value.

The question is, "Will more time give you more money?" The answer to this question is almost never yes. More time is not the issue. The issue is taking the time you do have and getting the important things done and delegating the rest to someone else. Once you do this, time is no longer an issue.

When I first started in real estate, I didn't have any time either. I was working sixteen hours a day. Previously, I had run service stations, and then, too, it seemed like I never had any time. Over the years, I realized I didn't have any time because I didn't make any time. I consciously started asking myself the same question I'm proposing you should ask yourself at every turn: "Is what I'm doing right now a valuable use of my time?"

To get your time in order, you first need a system for managing it and making sure the things you want to get done actually get done. For this to happen, your tasks must be part of a daily plan and always in front of you until they get done. I use a simple planner to do this. Yes, I'm talking about paper—you know, the stuff made from trees, the material that contains the words you're reading right now. Actual paper.

A planner not only helps me track the things I have to do but also eliminates the need for a good memory. If efficiency required memory, I wouldn't get anything done. A planner provides a place for me to write down ideas and notes and thoughts without ever losing a thing. A planner holds me accountable for keeping my promises. A planner holds others accountable for keeping their promises to me. A planner is, in short, a businessperson's best friend.

I'm not exaggerating when I say a planner is the difference between becoming a person who others look up to and want to follow because he does what he says and becoming an unorganized mess who breaks promises, losing the trust of everyone around him. Nobody buys the hot air people like this spout because they have a track record of not following up.

People ask me all the time how I get so much done. The answer is simple: I set it and forget it. I do this in my planner. Lots of people use electronic planners, and I'm okay with this. The problem is most people don't use them correctly. They just use little pieces of them. They collect only pieces of the information they need, and they remember only pieces of great ideas because they don't fully learn how to use their gadgets to manage their time.

You can buy a paper planner at any office store. Mine, like most, has several sections, and I'll describe how I use them here to help you if you decide to use a book. If you don't, I'll also discuss ways I use my iPhone to improve time management.

The first section of your planner is called "one through thirty-one," or your daily to-do list. I use a planner called "Time Keeper," but any good one will work. Back in the eighties, I used a Franklin Day Planner, and those are still available. All planners have a place to put your to-do list and your daily activities, usually with a schedule of particular days, where you can write down your appointments, tasks, and the like. Putting the things you need to get done down on particular days will force you to create deadlines, too, a key step in making progress. If you're not willing to put yourself under pressure by creating self-imposed deadlines, then you can't bitch when you don't become a super-achiever.

This is the easy part of your planner. Anybody can write down things to do and check them off when they're done, as I do daily. Also, this is the most important part of the planner. Until an item hits this daily to-do list, it's not going to get done. Tasks must be in front of you, written out on the day when they need to get done.

When I say, "set it and forget it," the goal is to get a task on my daily to-do list so when I open my planner in the morning, it's right in front of me all day. Over the course of the day, I systematically work to check off those to-do items and try to get them all done before my day is over. The challenge, of course, is I'm adding items as well as checking them off. Sure, it's two steps forward, one step back, but putting items in the planner keeps them right in front of me, so I never neglect or forget them.

Most people know what a to-do list is and have some version of one. These days, many keep to-do lists in their phone. But do you keep your phone open to the to-do list—is it in front of you all the time? The answer is probably no, because inevitably, you're using the phone for other tasks. A planner exists for one reason—for its owner to review throughout the day until all items are checked off.

Also in any planner is a monthly "calendar at a glance." This is pretty valuable to me because my to-do list is only for the month in question. If we're in the month of November, there will only be thirty pages in my to-do list because there are only thirty days in

November. Hence, I can only work one month at a time on my to-do list. We also need a place to schedule things out that are not in the month we're in and currently working on. This is where the monthly planner comes in handy.

The monthly planner is usually large enough to make small notes. For example, if I'm working in November and I want to write down something that needs to get done or an appointment that needs to be kept in December, then I can turn to my monthly calendar and put it in the December calendar. Then, when I get to December's to-do list, the one through thirty-one, I transfer the items from the monthly to the daily. From this point on, I can "set it and forget it" because they're listed on the day when I intend to take action on them.

I know this all sounds a little trite and childish, but I can tell you, this habit alone will make or break your time-management skills. Simple as it sounds, most people will not follow the advice I just gave. Instead, they try to remember everything. I don't think I have to tell you how flawed this approach to time management is.

All planners also come with an "A through Z," which is a place where you can keep contact information for important people, or at least those important enough to make it to your planner. It's the equivalent of the "contacts" button on your telephone but offers a distinct advantage, which I'll explain below.

In the back of all good planners is a page called "information manager" or "contact manager" or "communication recap" or something similar. Almost no one uses this little-known item, which can really make you stand out as a thoroughly organized person. The information manager has a place for the contact information of important people in your life at the top, and it also has a place for you to make a note every time you have a conversation with that important person.

How do you use this feature? Well, if, for example, I was hiring a contractor to renovate a house, I'd have an information manager listing for my contractor. Every time I had a conversation with this contractor, I'd make a little note in my information manager. The next time I was on the phone with him, I would refer back to notes from all the conversations we had. This allows me to hold him accountable for every promise he's made—and to make him believe I've got the memory of an elephant.

Let's say my contractor's name is John Smith and he has a daughter named Melissa. Melissa was in a soccer tournament coming up the weekend after I last talked to John. I just made a note: Melissa soccer tournament. When I next get John on the phone, I'll say, "Hey, John, did Melissa win the tournament?" John will think I'm a genius. He will think I remember everything. In reality, I'm just reading the note I made from the last conversation.

By being the one who keeps notes on important conversations with important people in your life, you will definitely stand out. They will know you are going to hold them accountable because they think you have the kind of memory power very few of us actually have. This is where the A through Z feature, or contact log, is key to the system. For example, when it comes to John the contractor, I have a choice: I can file his information manager under C for contractor or S for Smith, whichever I think I'll get to the quickest. Either way, the next time John calls or I call him, I quickly flip to his information manager. Instantly, I'll have access to all the conversations we've had—I don't have to remember anything.

I use this same planner to keep track of important things. For example, every year we have a real estate event, The Great American Real Estate Summit. My planner has note sheets that replace the yellow pads many people carry around. One of those I've titled

"Summit." Actually, there are three called "Summit" because this is how much space I need for the ideas I have about the event.

When an idea occurs to me, I don't have to remember it. I just turn to the S in my phone log, find the summit sheet, and make a note on it. When I'm ready to take action on the summit sheets, I review them. Then the key, of course, is anything requiring action must be transferred from my note pages or my information manager to my daily one through thirty-one. I'll put it down on the day when I think I'll get this task done.

When I open my planner on that day, there it is right in front of me. The task will get done before I leave my desk. If it does not get done before I leave for the day, then I will have to write it in the next day's to-do list. This forces me to complete the project because I grow antsy to get it out of my book. I know it's a simple thing, but it really works.

Also in my planner, I have a page called "Ideas." Sometimes I just get an idea and I don't know what to do with it in the moment, but I don't want to lose it. I never do. I open my planner and write the idea down, filed under "I" for ideas. Then I review the ideas from time to time. It's just amazing how many of the items I see in my planner with checkmarks beside them used to be ideas and then became reality. Following this system will require a habit change. You must do things a little differently than you have been, but it's not a major change. The largest habit you'll have to adopt is to start writing things down. Most people simply won't stop and do this. If I'm in a conversation with you and I hear or think of something worthy of writing down, I'll stop the conversation and write it on something right then and there. I won't let the conversation continue because I know if I wait, the idea is gone. The older I get, the faster the ideas seem to go.

Today, I also often use the Reminder app, which comes with most mobile phones. Instead of writing something down, I just punch up Siri and say, "Siri, remind me to . . . _____." The problem with this is if I don't take the reminder note when it pops up and stick it in my planner so the action gets taken, then obviously nothing is going to happen with it. It will just be another reminder sitting on my app forever. It comes back to transferring everything you want done into your planner, and when applicable, transferring it to the one through thirty-one.

In the old days, I carried a pen and paper everywhere. Today, you'll still never see me without a pen, but I also rely heavily on my Reminder app. Sometimes it's just not convenient to use a pen and paper. Along with the Reminder app, I also use the Notes app included with my telephone. This is especially true since I discovered all I have to do is tell Siri to write a note for me, and she'll do it while I'm talking into the telephone. Instead of me having to pull out a pencil and paper, I just tell Siri to either make me a reminder in my Reminder app or to write a note in my Notes app. Again, for the system to work, I have to make sure this info ultimately gets into my planner.

I also use the Calendar app included in my phone. All of the events I'll teach are in it. However, I find this inadequate to replace the calendar in my planner. In my planner, I get to make little notes on any day of the month I want to do something, up to three years in advance.

Another advantage of the book is that it's a lot faster than the cell phone. I can write something in my book faster than I can even get onto my cell phone. My daily plan is in front of me all day long in my planner, staring me in the face, while I have to roam around for such info on my cell phone. Typing a note into my cell phone takes far longer than it does to write it into my planner.

You're probably thinking I'm archaic for carrying around a paper planner, but when you and I meet face to face, I'll show you why my planner far exceeds your cell phone in the art of time management. Yes, it's a book. Yes, I have to carry it. Yes, I could lose it. I haven't lost one since 1983, when I started using them, but it's possible. However, I can also scan important items from my planner into the cloud anytime.

Are you keeping your promises? Are you holding other people accountable for their promises to you by making notes in your planner to record them? Are you using your time productively by simply making decisions? People who don't make time to focus on the big decisions don't fare well.

Don't Be a Flattened Squirrel

At the very end of life, the highways are filled with flat squirrels who couldn't make a decision. And making decisions, I've learned, doesn't really take much time. The minutia is what takes the time. Are you keeping track of your great ideas? Can you find them even after you write them down?

Of course, all of the planners in the world won't help you if you're not delegating to others the tasks you currently perform. We will explore delegating in chapter 7 and outsourcing in chapter 8. If I can get you to think more about delegating and outsourcing and less about doing things yourself, and then perhaps inject some time management skills into your life, I've accomplished my mission in writing this book.

CHAPTER 6

Locating Prospects

Make Them Come to You

Any business must follow five steps in order to be successful, regardless of the product or service it sells:

> STEP 1: Locate prospects.
>
> STEP 2: Prescreen prospects.
>
> STEP 3: Construct and present offers.
>
> STEP 4: Follow up.
>
> STEP 5: Close quickly.

The step business owners ignore more than any other is Step 1, locate prospects. It amazes me the number of businesspeople who have no clue how to get customers. Most are pretty good at delivering the product or service they sell. Some come with many years of experience. But rarely do I talk with anyone who wants to discuss marketing. The general attitude is, "I don't know anything about marketing. It costs money and doesn't work." I'm here to tell you, it does work. Like everything worthwhile, it's an art, and it must be learned. I've spent several hundred million dollars on marketing in my career and continue to spend on it every day—in every business I operate.

In this book, I am discussing three businesses I own: a restaurant, a publishing company, and a real estate company that buys and sells houses. The restaurant is certainly a product business, but it's also a service business, as are the other two. These businesses are very different, but all three incorporate the five steps above and the hated thing called marketing.

Most small-business owners, at least the ones who run brick-and-mortar operations, think if you open it, customers will come. My question is, what if they don't? The answer is—such businesses will be closed shortly after they open. Before I buy or open any kind of business, I first want to know how I'm going to get customers for it. If I don't have an answer to this question, then there won't be any business.

Step 1 above is "locate prospects." If the business owner can't do this, the other four steps are irrelevant because the business will never get started. If it does get started, the business won't make it, because the owner is too lazy or intimidated to learn a little bit about marketing. I often say that if they took away all my skills and left me with only one, I would want it to be the ability to exchange my product or service for other people's money cost effectively. This, my friends, is marketing, and it's fundamental to growing your business.

There are three ways to grow a business internally:

1. Get more customers.

2. Get customers to spend more often.

3. Get customers to spend more per transaction.

All three of these strategies require marketing. The only kind of marketing I'll ever do is direct marketing. Why? Because direct marketing allows you to measure the results for every dollar you spend on it. If you can't measure the results, don't spend the dollars. Direct marketing provides a direct channel from your business to potential customers and can take many forms—email campaigns, online display ads, fliers, letters, targeted radio and TV commercials, and many more.

The key to direct marketing is building in a way to measure its results—an actionable element—such as a number to call, a coupon to mail in, a link to click. These built-in responses can be measured and tracked so you know exactly how effective your marketing is. If they aren't measured, you can only guess at what works or doesn't work and make decisions based on SWAG (scientific wild-ass guess). SWAG is common but not a very good business model. In all my years of marketing at my company, Global Publishing, with hundreds of marketing tests and millions of wasted dollars, we've learned one glaring lesson we try not to keep learning:

It Is a Fool Who Thinks He Is
Smarter than the Market

We learned the campaigns we thought were sure things were usually disappointing, and the ones we expected to do poorly sometimes became big hits. Sometimes we couldn't even figure out why. They just were. People are funny and fickle and hard to predict, so the only way to find out what works and what doesn't is to . . .

TEST, TEST, TEST.

Here's an example from my restaurant. We put discount coupons in our local edition of *Mint* magazine, a monthly book of discounts that is area specific, allowing us to choose homes close to us. We've tried several versions of the coupon:

- $10 off with purchase of $35

- $15 off with $50 purchase

- BOGO, buy one get one

- free appetizer with dinner

Okay, so which one do you think works best? Here are last month's results:

	Total Redeemed	Discounts	Cash Collected
$10 off	87	$977	$3,135
$15 off	109	$168	$6,278
BOGO	160	$2,440	$6,144
Free app	28	$331	$1,940

So the BOGO and the $15 off are the big winners, but how would we know that if we didn't carefully measure the results? This isn't rocket science. We simply stapled the coupons to the sales slips and physically calculated the results. What did they show? Well, every time we gave away a BOGO, which we capped at $15, the table spent an additional $38.40 on average. Our cost on the $15 is about $6, so that means we spent $6 to get $38—and likely a new customer. With the $15 off deal, the average check was $57.50 in cash collected. This means we got fewer customers, but the ones we did get are worth more, spend better, and will continue to do so if my staff doesn't piss them off first.

These two coupons survive the test, and the others go to failed-test heaven, where they'll have plenty of company.

Another popular form of marketing is "image advertising," which is very different from direct advertising or direct marketing. Big, dumb companies use image advertising. They really have no idea how their marketing is working. Their sales might go up a little, but this doesn't mean their marketing caused the increase. Yet they spend millions of dollars buying advertisements that mean absolutely nothing to the consuming public. Obviously, your business can't afford to do this. I know mine can't.

I want to know what effect was produced for every dollar spent. I want to know my numbers. I want to stand out from the clutter! What do I mean by this? In *Mint* magazine, we insert a slide-in coupon that is a half-page sticking over the top of the cover by about an inch. It has a headline like Free Dinner or Free Fillet, and it literally stands out. I don't want to be in a magazine with a hundred similar ads. I want to be the only slide-in. This way, I know everybody who picks up the magazine is going to read my coupon.

In my old restaurant, which was a steakhouse, we gave away a free fillet. If you saw the words "free fillet" sticking out of your local coupon magazine, would you read it? You would if you were a man. The catch was, in order to get the free fillet dinner, which was worth about $24, customers had to buy at least an additional $25 in food. It didn't take us long to figure out when we gave away a free fillet dinner, we collected $46 over and above the coupon cost.

Yes, we had to pay to put the coupons in the magazine, but since we collected $36 more than we gave away, we essentially got paid to acquire a customer. This, my friends, is the most important factor. We got paid to acquire a customer. There are many businesses, including my publishing company, that do not get paid to acquire customers. In fact, at Global Publishing, we go in the hole every time someone comes into our system for the first time.

In my restaurant, we have a VIP Club card on each table. The servers actually get paid to get our new customers to fill out the VIP Club card and join the club. The customer gets a free appetizer at a later visit for doing so. The VIP card gives us the contact information on customers, including their address, email, and cell phone number. In other words, we build a buyers list by giving away an appetizer.

Why is this important? Because now we know who our customers are. We have their contact information. We can use that information to get them to buy more often and to spend more per transaction. Without this information, we have no idea who our customers are, which is the case with most restaurants. I wonder why they have trouble getting customers to come back.

I am appalled at businesses selling products or services and not collecting the information on who their customers are. Without a database such as this, approximately half of our restaurant revenue would not exist. Once you start a relationship, you must cultivate it. This includes giving customers a shameless bribe to come back and do business with you again and more often. The bribe can't be delivered if we don't know who to send it to. Tracking this info and running a coupon campaign is not difficult. Our participation is simply to say how many coupons we want to put out and where. For Iggy's, this means a five-mile radius from the restaurant. We decide our target area, make a phone call, and we're done. No work or minutia, so any owner or manager can do it.

Our participation in the VIP Club campaign is minimal, too. Servers simply make diners aware of the offer in front of them on the table. Small work, big results—and most important, all of the results are measurable and on autopilot. It's true some people will find their way to the restaurant without the coupons and without any advertising, but I'm not going to leave it to chance.

Now, let's look at Global Publishing. We have a sixty-second commercial on the radio almost every day, giving away my free book and CD on how to buy and sell houses without using money or credit. (You can get it at www.ronsfreebook.com or 800-870-4365.)

The customers who call to get the free book and CD are immediately upsold to a $29 item and from there, to a $97 item while on the telephone. They call an interactive voice response system, or IVR, which works twenty-four hours a day with no human intervention. Note the automation. The IVR takes the credit card numbers of customers—at least, the 10 percent of them who actually buy something—and drops them into the system. Then an outsourced company takes all that information off the IVR and sends it to us daily. Every time a customer spends $29 or $97 with us, we go in the hole about $100 to acquire the customer. Why, you ask, would we go in the hole to acquire a customer?

The answer is simple. Within a few months of our acquiring such customers, they have spent on average about $300 with us. Would you spend $100 to get back $300 three months later and then have a customer for life? Most businesses won't because they simply haven't taken time to understand marketing, and they aren't willing to invest the money upfront to get those valuable customers. They're intimidated by something that is actually fairly easy. Running these radio ads, for instance, requires one email per week. A "radio buyer" does all the placement. We don't even know where they're running; we just know the results. That's it. After these leads come in, my team follows up to get them to spend money over the next few months and years.

Next, let's talk about the business of buying and selling houses. This is a business you should like because it applies to you regardless of the business you're in. Given a little time to explore real estate, you'll want to get involved in it, if you aren't already.

There are two sides to the real estate business. We have to find sellers, and we have to find buyers. In the "pretty house" side of our business, which involves beautiful homes in beautiful neighborhoods, we're dealing with the owners of the properties, not Realtors or banks. That's about 90 percent of my current business. It is absolutely on autopilot, to the point where it only takes a few hours of my time per month. Almost all of this business is accomplished by virtual assistants and outsourcing.

To find sellers, we only have to do a few things. Our virtual assistant locates them online from ads, calls them, and fills out a property information sheet. Sellers respond by email and/or phone. If they respond by email, the message goes right to the virtual assistant, who then fills out the property information sheet. If sellers respond by phone, we use a company called PATLive (www.patlive.com/ron-legrand), which takes their inbound call twenty-four hours a day and then sends the information to us. From there, it goes to the virtual assistant, who still fills out a property information sheet for each caller.

I also teach my students how to get people to ride around and look for signs advertising houses "For Sale by Owner." The people scouting these signs snap a picture when they spot one, then send the pic to my students, who forward them to their VAs, who fill out the property information sheet. The process I just described is in itself enough to run any real estate business and provide more leads than its operator can handle.

Think about it: all of the work I just described is done by the virtual assistant or PATLive—none by the student. When my students get the property information sheet, they only have to make one phone call. This comes after the virtual assistant has prescreened the seller to determine whether he or she is interested in "terms" or not. About one-third of them say they would consider terms, which means lease option or seller financing.

My student makes one phone call using my scripts, sets the appointment, and then goes to the house and gets the contract signed. That's his total participation up to this point, after he has set the systems up. The cost overall for getting a completed property information sheet, including the VA services, is about $25 per lead. Depending on the skill of the student, he or she will take those leads and convert about one out of ten or fifteen into a deal. The minimum deal I'll allow any of my students to make includes a $10,000 net profit. This profit is usually achieved within the first thirty days, and that's only the upfront money.

Many deals also have a sizable monthly income, the difference between the rent collected and the payment to the seller. Sometimes this gap exceeds $1,000 per house. Then there's the backend profit, when the tenant-buyer gets financing months later and cashes us out. These profits can exceed $100,000. All of this profit comes without risk, credit, capital, licensing, or costly entanglements.

Would you spend a few hundred a month to have leads located for you and most of the work done knowing there was a $10,000 check waiting a few days later? That's exactly what my students have been doing since we incorporated automation, systemization, and outsourcing into their lives. I discovered a long time ago that sellers won't find their way to me simply because I want them to. I actually have to let them know I buy houses to make this happen, and today this work is done for me.

In selling houses, we do two things. Our VAs run ads online after creating a flyer to drive traffic to the house, and we have a local assistant who puts a sign out front. All the inbound calls go into our IVR system (a sophisticated voicemail system) twenty-four hours a day, with no humans involved. Our virtual assistants take the information off the IVR and call back the buyers who are worth following up. The VAs then alert the student about which leads need to be contacted. It's all automatic.

The student's job is to tell us to set up the IVR. After this, he or she simply waits for the VA to say which of the people coming through have enough money down to make them worth calling back. The student just decides which person he wants to try to put in a house. Since our houses are mostly sold with terms, the down payment or the nonrefundable option deposit is the top-qualifying criterion, not credit.

Most of the people I put into homes are not creditworthy. They can't go down to the bank and get a loan. In fact, about 80 percent of people shopping for homes today can't get loans. All of them, however, can be qualified over time, so we put them in houses on a lease-purchase agreement, buy them time, and help them fix what's broke. Ultimately, this leads them to a bank to get new loans. It all starts with marketing, automation, and systemization getting them into our system.

Let me say it again: all marketing must be measurable, or you shouldn't spend money on it. If you can't quantify the results, then don't spend the money. If you have a brick-and-mortar business, you'll get pressure from advertising people of all sorts wanting you to run ads on radio, Internet, TV, and print. All of these formats work, but all of them must also be measured.

I also use social media—Facebook, Twitter, and the like—to reach customers, and you should, too. My advice, however, is to hire professionals who really know their stuff. It's smarter to spend a little with those who know the craft than to spend more money trying to learn it yourself—and never doing as good a job as the expert. It takes time and focus to learn the art of Internet marketing. Most people running a business will never devote the necessary time and focus to it. And once you learn it, you have to relearn it because it's changing constantly.

Don't Try to Master Your Weaknesses, Delegate Them!

In my restaurant, I hire a media company to handle all my emails, social media, and graphics for a few hundred dollars a month. In my real estate business, my marketing costs are small because I don't need many customers. The Internet is an important component for me in these and other companies, but a company marketing solely on the Internet is missing at least half of the business it could get by using other media as well. Only 5 to 20 percent of people on any email list you're mailing will ever open your email. This is not true when I circulate a coupon, postcard, or letter. Most consumers will get those and open and read them. To send an email, you must first acquire people's email addresses and get their permission to send it. You don't have these requirements for any other media.

Regardless of your product, service, business, or profession is, it's your job to make the world know your products and services are available. If you don't do that job, then your business will suffer. You will suffer. Your family will suffer because you didn't take a little time to learn about marketing.

CHAPTER 7

Delegation Nation

Anything You Can Do, They Can Do Better

I've mentioned delegation as well as outsourcing already. They might seem like the same thing, but there's actually a big difference between the two. Delegation means you're assigning tasks to people who work for you or with you, such as your employees or your personal assistant. Outsourcing means the task is done outside your organization by someone who is not your employee but is available for hire. We'll cover outsourcing in the next chapter. This chapter is all about getting the help you'll need for everything you don't outsource to other companies or to virtual assistants. If you're using a virtual assistant, you're outsourcing. If you're using a personal assistant, you're delegating. Delegating is "in-house," and outsourcing is "out of house."

If you'll recall, in chapter 1, I asked you to get out of your own way, and I said the only way you'll be able to do this is to delegate as much of what you currently do to others as soon as possible. In my opinion, if you don't develop this habit, then you'll never be truly free and take control of your time and your life. You simply can't be all things to all people. You must learn to let others do what they do best and get out of their way, and do what you do best: make decisions. You can't do everything and get anywhere—no more than a rat running in a circular cage can ever reach a destination, no matter how hard he runs. I guess you could say, it's delegate or die.

Have you delegated enough? Well, ask yourself, can you take time off and go on a vacation and have your business run without you? If you get sick and laid up for a month, will your business survive? It takes a real storm in your life to make you realize how much worrying you've done over the squalls. Don't sweat the small stuff. In 2009, I had a quadruple bypass. I was in the hospital for five days and then at home on strict bed rest, for a total of thirty days off work. Most brick-and-mortar businesses would suffer greatly or go out of business if the owner took off a month. But if you can't take off a month and have your business run without you, you need serious help delegating.

Delegating frees up time, allowing you to play your proper role in your business: making decisions, generating new revenue sources, and focusing on the big picture. You can't focus on the big picture if you're always part of the picture. The next question is, "To whom do you delegate?" Of course, the answer is going to vary greatly depending on the business or industry you're in, but most businesses have the same types of tasks that have to get done day in and day out.

The most important person in your business, when you're ready for him or her, is a personal assistant. Anyone running a business of any size needs a personal assistant. I wouldn't be without one. In fact, I've always joked, when I check into the nursing home, I want my PA nearby in case I actually come back to my senses and have something I want to get done. The personal assistant is the absolute key to mastering delegation.

Since they're so important, let's start by answering a few questions concerning personal assistants and see how you might benefit from using one in your life and business. First, when do you need a PA? Well, my answer is, as soon as you can afford one and decide you want to be free. If you're running a business that is generating more than a quarter of a million dollars a year in revenue, you need a PA. If you have other employees but don't have a PA, a PA should be next on your list. Perhaps one of your current employees would be good in this position.

The first biggest question on everybody's mind when considering a PA is, "Can I afford one?" Well, let's take a look at cost. You can get a good PA anywhere in America for between $30,000 and $45,000 per year. I'll come back to what their qualifications should be in a minute, but I can tell you, I travel all over the country—and $30,000 to $45,000 will hire a good person to do everything you need a PA to do. Can you pay them more? Certainly, but you can also get them for less.

There are a lot of folks out there right now looking for full-time jobs who have ideal qualifications to be personal assistants. You might be thinking, "Well, gosh, that's a lot of money." Is it? It breaks down to about $3,000 a month. The bigger question is, "If you hired a PA full-time, would the PA generate at least enough income to cover his or her cost?" If the answer is no, then you're certainly not ready for a PA. However, I suspect by the time we get through with this conversation, you'll realize the cost of the PA, while not irrelevant, becomes insignificant because having this person is so very important to your ability to grow your business. Nothing will go further in freeing you up from the minutia.

Do you have to have an office to have a PA? Absolutely not. My PA, for years, worked out of her home while I worked in an office. Today, my PA, Tish, works ten feet from me but only when I'm in the office. Since I'm on the road so much, it really doesn't make any difference whether my office is ten feet or a thousand miles away from her. Tish will do the same task. With today's technology and communication, you can be anywhere and have a PA anywhere, and I know a lot of people who have long-distance PAs. However, if you have an office, this is probably where you want your PA. I'm in an office and personally, much prefer my PA and other employees to be there with me. But again, in today's virtual world, it's not a requirement—just my preference.

What would a PA do for you? Well, let me first say what mine does for me, and then we'll talk about what yours can do for you. Tish pretty much runs all of my businesses except Global Publishing, VA Services, and Gold Club; Jennifer Shedlin runs those. Tish plays a stronger role in some than in others, but she plays a role in all of them.

When it comes to my restaurant, for example, Tish communicates with the general manager and handles some of the reporting. She checks the reporting I get from the restaurant but also creates some reports we just decided to do in-house on our own. She does a lot of research for the restaurant, assessing vendors, equipment, products, and the like. She doesn't work in the business—she claims no apron will fit her, and I doubt I'll ever catch her in the back washing dishes—but she acts as a watchdog over it. Her role in running the restaurant is vital to me because if she didn't do the tasks she was assigned, they would fall on me. And I've got to tell you, if I had to do them, there very well might not be a restaurant.

At Global Publishing, our COO, Jennifer, has a PA of her own to whom she assigns the day-in and day-out tasks necessary to run a sixty-employee multimillion-dollar company. As you can imagine, there is a never-ending list of things that must be done every single day to market and deliver our seminars, products, and services to our vast customer base all across North America.

Since Jennifer runs Global, there's very little for Tish to do there, but she is the liaison between me and most Global matters. Yes, I communicate with Jennifer on a regular basis. We usually have one or two meetings per week lasting anywhere from five minutes to an hour. And these meetings are always in the afternoon because I rarely show up before the crack of noon.

In my real estate business, Tish does everything that the virtual assistants don't do. This includes talking to all of our potential buyers after they've been screened through our IVR system, at least the ones with money. She generates reports about both buyers and sellers. She keeps track of the information collected on sellers by our virtual assistants and makes sure they are getting called by the person to whom I've outsourced the job of setting up appointments to get contracts. Tish handles the contractors from beginning to end when we do rehabs. She handles real estate agents, too, because we actually list the properties we renovate with Realtors when we're ready to sell them.

You might be thinking, "But Ron, you let her handle your contractors?" The answer is, absolutely. First of all, she's a woman. Most men have no business picking out colors or decorating anything. Women buy houses, and most women are better than most men in deciding such matters, so what good am I?

Second, she knows what the house should look like when it's finished better than I do. Why do I need to stick my nose in it? If she says it's ready to sell, it's ready to sell. She's much pickier than I am.

Third, managing contractors to renovate houses is a small task to her. Tish literally managed thirty-two commercial projects in nine states simultaneously back when I was heavily buying commercial properties with my students. She didn't manage each project, but she managed the managers of the projects. This job required her to take trips without me to various cities where I had deals in the works and to conduct meetings when I wasn't present. A personal assistant who can accomplish these sorts of tasks is one who can easily replace you, if you decide you'll let him or her. Believe me, handling contractors to renovate houses is a small task for a PA as good as Tish. It doesn't even take much of her time, because a typical renovation only involves two to three trips to the house during the entire process.

Now, I'll say, most of the time, I actually visit the contractor to create the initial repair list. And lately, I'm only doing this with her by my side, so I don't have to do it in the future. Sometimes I visit the property after it's completed if I happen to be nearby but not always. The point is, like most of my business tasks, this entire process is delegated to my PA. Yes, it took a while to create a relationship like the one Tish and I have—and to train her to think for me and like me. Getting her to the point where she can make decisions on 90 percent of the things that come her way, so I don't have to, took some work. But ask yourself, "What would a person like this be worth in my life?" The answer is, certainly more than $30,000 to $45,000 a year. In fact, I wish I could get Tish to work for this. She currently makes more money than many corporate executives, but then again, she essentially is a corporate executive.

The next question is, "What would I have this personal assistant do in my particular business?" To answer this, make a list of everything you do on a daily basis and assign everything you can force yourself to let go of to a personal assistant. Do this gradually, once you've had them in the system for a couple of months and you feel they're going to stay. Start assigning tasks little by little and watch what happens. If you have the right PA, you'll discover he or she is a lot smarter than you think.

PAs can do a lot more than you imagine. Most want you to give them more work—boredom is the worst killer of a PA–boss relationship. Tish will be the first to tell you she's never bored. If she were, she probably wouldn't still be around. The only way you can kill boredom and create relationships where your employees will do things without you standing over them with a whip is if you give them some independence and get out of their way. Yes, this even means letting them make mistakes until they learn to do a job correctly. If you delegate in this way, you'll quickly have an amazing revelation: "Gosh, I should have done this years ago. The world will survive without me and my hands in every little thing."

Make the list of everything you wish you could get done daily, and add it to the list of everything you currently do. Assign most of it to your personal assistant, and then you can stand back and work on your business, grow your revenue, and grow more income streams. You can get out of the way and make decisions, as you should.

What traits do you need in a PA? It's a key question. Of course, you want to surround yourself with capable people.

If You Surround Yourself with Dummies, You Just Get Bad Decisions More Quickly

Well, here's a simple way to remember the traits to look for in your PA: Cab Co., C-A-B-C-O. CABCO stands for communication, attitude, brain, computer skills, and only one boss (that's you—they can't have another job and be your PA; it never works). PAs are the link between you and all the folks you work with. Their communication skills are critical. They represent you, and if they actually become your customer-prevention department, they need to be replaced or fixed quickly.

Attitude is the biggest thing I look for in all employees because without the right attitude, I can't fix them. With a good attitude, we can train them to do anything that needs to be done. However, I wouldn't hire a PA who needed training in computer skills. Anybody applying for a PA job should have computer skills or should look for work elsewhere. College credentials certainly are not required for a good PA—brains are. Many of the smartest people I know didn't go to college. In fact, a college degree might just get in the way.

Make a list of everything you want a PA to do because if you don't know, your PA certainly won't. If you use a temp service to find your PA, this is the first thing they're going to ask: "What requirements do you have for a PA?" At the bottom of this list, the last line should always be "any other task assigned by management." That's your escape clause in case one says to you, "Well, this wasn't in my job description." Your answer? "Yes, look at the bottom. Everything is in your job description."

Once this list of tasks is created and it's time to interview candidates for a PA position, I always make them read the list back to me to make sure they understand it and are interpreting in the same way I am. It's amazing, when you have people vocalize things, how big the gap can be between what you said and what they heard. Finally, I have them sign off on a statement at the bottom of the page, saying they've made a commitment, they understand the list, and they can handle the list. Without this list, my friend, you can't create accountability. Without accountability, you'll always have a mess. So to recap: make the list, go over the list, and get the list signed.

If you don't feel you can handle a PA at this time because the money scares you, I have to ask, "Isn't this the very reason you need to get more income in your life? Isn't this why you are at the point where you can't hire a PA? What's wrong? What are you doing incorrectly?" I'm willing to bet the answers revolve around all the minutia sucking up your time, which, in turn, is probably the reason your income is too low to hire a PA.

It's a vicious circle, but remember, the cost of PAs is insignificant as long as they help you make more revenue than they cost. People complain about having employees. Well, I love employees, but I expect them to make more than they cost. I'd take ten thousand employees if each and every one of them was making ten times more than they cost.

If you run a service business—dentistry, medicine, accounting, law—you should already have a personal assistant, but if you don't, how many new clients do you need to cover a PA's cost? How much more time can be freed up to focus on serving your most important clients, making decisions, and growing revenue? PAs can always be on the telephone if they run out of office work. There are always customers and clients who need calls. There's always something you can have them doing to generate more revenue and better serve your clients. If you're an online business, the tasks are endless. Online businesses require continual research—one of a good PA's prime functions. Are there more items you should be selling?

Can your PA help you discover which ones? If you run an online business, you should decide what you're going to sell, create the copy to sell it, and have others do the rest. Most online marketers I know, and I know many, work from their homes. Their heads are always in the copy, adding more products and upselling to existing customers. One of the laziest Internet marketers I know is Brian Hanson, who lives on the beach in Jacksonville, Florida. He has more than three hundred websites, and he's never built one in his life. Everything he does is outsourced. He even has virtual assistants to manage his virtual assistants. He's the laziest man on the Internet for a reason—and he's my hero.

Business owners who are worried about the cost of a PA often ask me if they should hire a part-time personal assistant. Do you really not have enough going on to keep a full-time assistant busy? If not, you probably don't need a PA. But if you're running a brick-and-mortar business, a retail business, and your PA hits a lull, can you put him or her on the telephone to solicit business? If you run a restaurant, can the PA call your clients and make them a special offer? Can your PA distribute coupons to businesses surrounding the restaurant? Can they call companies and book parties?

This approach applies to any business. If you're running a real estate agency, most of what you do can be assigned to a personal assistant. All the grunt work, secretarial work, unscreened calls—all of the timewasters currently weighing on your life—can be assigned to someone else for a small amount of money. Are you telling me you can't get one or two more listings, or one or two more sales, to cover the cost of your PA? If you spend the money on a PA and don't start earning more than the PA costs, then you're not using your time productively.

Can you picture Donald Trump or Warren Buffett typing their own letters, taking unscreened calls, or doing any of the things we all do day in and day out which we shouldn't be doing? Of course not, but they're also using the time they save wisely—delegating, so they can focus on increasing revenue. As I've written many times and will continue to write in coming chapters, building revenue is your real job. Delegating is key to making this happen, and so is outsourcing, which we'll explore in the next chapter.

CHAPTER 8

Bring Outsourcing In

Finding Companies That Can Do It All

If you'll recall, delegating means you're assigning tasks to people in your organization, either an employee, personal assistant, or someone else on your payroll. Outsourcing means the job is being done by a company or a person outside your organization, someone who is not on your payroll. I use outsourcing more and more in all of my businesses. Our society runs virtually these days, allowing you to get things done all over the world, literally at the touch of a button. There are endless people who'll gladly do any task for you, quickly and competently for a paltry amount of money. There are websites where you can arrange to have tasks performed, often for pennies. You'll be amazed at what you can get done if you take the time to explore the possibilities.

In my businesses, I use outsourcing for almost everything that I can get done outside of the building. It's sometimes cheaper, but even if it isn't, outsourcing lowers the level of pressure inside the building and ensures the consistent completion of tasks. If an outside company doesn't complete a task, it gets replaced, and the workers know it. If I assign a task to an inside person and it doesn't get completed, it's just another mission that got sidetracked and fell victim to minutia. Jobbing it out ensures focus. That doesn't mean they always get done, but it does mean we don't have to hire, train, or monitor the people doing it.

In my real estate business, my incoming calls from sellers responding to our ads go directly to a company called PATLive (www.PatLive.com/ronlegrand). This is a twenty-four-hour answering service that takes our calls, asks respondents a few questions, and then sends the information to our clients. Our clients forward the info to our virtual assistants so they can call the sellers who have suitable homes for sale. The process occurs twenty-four hours a day, and I don't even know the calls are taking place until I get the property information sheets completed. This service costs just $150 a month for 250 minutes of a live human being taking phone calls, which is obviously much cheaper than you could hire someone to do it. More important than cost is the fact no one you hire would be available twenty-four hours a day to take these calls.

We also mail letters to home sellers. We call them "yellow letters" because they're on yellow paper and look like they're handwritten. I introduced this program into the real estate industry about thirteen years ago, and it has become the number-one method ever created to get sellers to call you. The letters have proved incredibly effective, and the good news is, we don't even touch them. The letters are handled by Christy King of www.yellowletterlady.com. She performs every task required to get these letters in the mail to homeowners. She works off rented lists of homeowners, which can be segmented to target the market we wish to enter. Christy prints and addresses the letters and does a great job with them. They look personal, which is why they have a 100 percent open rate. Our job is simply to tell Christy how many to mail and when and then to pay her. She does everything else.

We don't call buyers either. Virtual assistants perform this task for us. Even though we own the virtual assistant firm, I have to pay the company the same as if it was someone else's (I probably should have a talk with my COO about that one).

Contractors do all of our repairs. I don't own a pickup truck to haul stuff. I used to. I had all the equipment required to renovate houses, a warehouse full of stuff, because I thought I was saving money. Well, I realized one day that the stuff I had in the warehouse was usually not the right stuff. If I did have the right stuff, it was buried when I needed it, and we had to buy it anyway. The equipment kept getting stolen or breaking. It had to be maintained and replaced. I came to realize over a period of years that I didn't want or need to be in the contracting business; I just needed to hire contractors. Now, we get a bid accepted, and we write three checks, and that's it. This is the sum total of our involvement in renovating houses. All the work is outsourced to contractors.

In the restaurant business, all of our social media and emailing and graphics needs are outsourced to one company. Our cleaning is outsourced, as well as our bookkeeping. At Global Publishing, we have numerous things being outsourced, but the one that probably merits the most discussion here is the purchase of radio media. We run sixty-second radio spots all over the country, almost every day. The radio ads offer a free book and CD and drive callers into our voice-response system. The voice system takes callers' information and tries to upsell them to a $29 and then a $97 product, so we can call them customers. They're customers the minute they give us money. If we had to use someone in-house to buy this radio time, we would first have to employ people who knew how to buy media, which is a skilled craft. You can't just hire people and train them to be good media buyers without some serious pain. It would require two to three employees to do the job we now accomplish with one email to our media buyer.

The media buyer decides where to run the ads, monitors where they should go based on past results (ours and similar companies'), tracks the results, reports the results, and gets discounts on advertising because of the volume they buy. Sure, we pay the professional media buyers 15 percent of the media cost, but we save more than this through the lower rates they get us and their ability to locate the best media with the best results for our products.

There was a time when we tried to do all of this in-house, which is why we now outsource it. We learned the hard way. What are you doing in-house that can be outsourced? Let's suppose you want some task done, either online or by telephone. My favorite online source for such jobs is www.fiverr.com. It's amazing what people will do for small amounts of money. I suggest you go on Fiverr.com and take some time to browse around. Perhaps you have some task you would like to get folks to come back and bid on. Simply tell them what you want done, and they'll tell you what they want to charge. You'll be shocked at how small the fees are.

Another good website is www.upwork.com, which used to be Elance. Fiverr and Upwork are loaded with people looking for work they can do from home. If you need it done and it can be accomplished online or by telephone, they almost always can do it.

Need a book written? Try www.textbroker.com. For $150, you can have a book in three days. Textbroker specializes in copywriting—sales letters, marketing materials, memos, manuals, web content. Whatever you need composed of words, somebody on this site can produce for a small amount money.

For web design, there's www.99designs.com. This company builds websites that work, and they do it cheaply. Having someone on your staff do what 99designs does would likely cost you several times more than they charge, and your staffer's work will probably need to be done a second time or fixed later. If you need content for a website or have other jobs that can be freelanced, www.freelancer.com is full of people looking for work and is loaded with valuable contacts. Need an animated video for your website or business? A site called www.goanimate.com creates affordable professional videos, the kind of stuff that fifteen years ago would have cost $5,000 to make. If browsing at GoAnimate sounds like a hassle, then go to fiverr.com and find someone who'll get on GoAnimate for you and get the video done. Get the idea? Even outsourcing can be outsourced!

And this, my friends, is the whole gist of this conversation. If you don't want to do it, or you can't do it, go to one of the sites in this book or others you know of and get someone who'll do it for you. This does not mean you're cutting corners or shirking work. In many cases, you can find people who'll do a better job than you or your employee would have because they have more experience and training in a particular area. The task you need done is their specialty. And because they have efficient systems in place and do a great volume, they can often do it cheaper than you. Don't try to master the things you're not good at—outsource them!

If you need ads run, web pages built, copy written, secretarial work done, etc. there's a website with people on it who are happy to exchange a small amount of your money for a large amount of their time—and they'll do a better job than you. Of course, someone actually must go on these sites and research them—and this would be a good job for a personal assistant. If a personal assistant is out of the question, then you can get a virtual assistant to do the same work for less money than you would spend going to dinner. In the last chapter, I argued strongly for hiring a personal assistant. I'm a big advocate of PAs; however, this is another employee and a fixed expense. It's an expense well worth incurring, but outsourcing is not a fixed expense and can be used as needed. You'll pay by the job, or by the minute, if you're using a virtual assistant, and this will cut your manpower costs considerably. The expertise needed to run most any business is varied, and no one person can be good at all the tasks outsourcers excel at. Most of the freelancers and outsource companies you'll contact do one or a few things very well. It just makes sense to use their expertise rather than training someone or having him learn as he goes. If your task is to climb a tree, do you want to train a horse or hire a squirrel?

Today, you have many choices for virtual assistants. A site called www.onlinejobs.ph has the best virtual assistants in the Philippines. In my experience, Filipino VAs do a very good job. Most speak fluent English, if you need them on the telephone, and they're very inexpensive. You can't get anything done in America for the price they'll charge in the Philippines.

If you're a real estate investor and you want a VA to do all the tasks involved in buying and selling houses, then you'll find no better service than Eagle VA, my in-house virtual assistant operation, available at www.ronlegrand.com. These VAs are trained to deal with sellers and buyers and focus strictly on real estate investors' needs. I created Eagle VA specifically to help our clients get through all the daily tasks they used to neglect or waste whole days on. My COO, Jennifer, came to me one day and said we couldn't fix the minutia problem unless we created our own virtual assistant company. The outside firms weren't doing the job we needed to get done, mainly calling sellers. Against my advice (I dreaded creating a giant daycare center), we built the company. I'm glad we did. This service has helped our clients to make a lot more money than they would have if left on their own to handle all the day to day details of business. The phone number for Global Publishing is 904-262-0491 if you wish to talk to someone about our VA service.

Some of our clients have attempted to hire VAs who'll work for less money, but they quickly reach the conclusion that cheaper is not always better. When you hire our VA service, you're hiring multiple VAs, each selected to do the job you assign him because it's what he's best at. For example, VAs who'll call FSBOs, for sale by owners, and complete a property information sheet are a specialized, highly trained group that do nothing but this day in and day out. This is why they're so good at it. It's hard work. Not everyone is cut out to call people and collect this sort of information, and if you give them anything else to do, of course they'll gravitate to the easier task. We have other VAs who research the ads online and turn them over to our callers, and we have still other VAs who specialize in running ads, building flyers, managing websites, calling buyers, and performing various other tasks involved in running our clients' businesses.

The point is, multiple VAs do a much better job than one VA when there are multiple tasks required. And our penny-pinching clients quickly find out, once their outside VA is gone, because he or she wasn't cut out for the job, that they have to start all over and train other VAs to do the same thing. This never happens with Eagle VA, because even though we lose people occasionally, trained replacements are always ready to step in, so there's no gap in production. Before you contact our office and ask, our virtual assistant company only works for real estate investors. Like most outsource companies, we know what we're good at and made the decision to focus on serving our particular clients instead of trying to be all things to all people.

There are highly trained and efficient specialists out there that could save you time and money, so even if you're skeptical, explore these resources. Consider which ones you could use and test them out. It costs nothing to tell people the kind of a job you want done and then read their replies. In fact, many of these freelancers work so cheaply, why not hire two or three to do the same job and then take the best of the three? You'll still pay less than you would to do the work in-house, and you can be assured of getting the best possible people for the job.

If you don't see a resource you like in the back of the book, there's always Google. Simply type your task into the search engine and up will pop pages of people and companies to complete it for you. How did we ever get along before Google, anyway?

CHAPTER 9

Why Real Estate?

You Really Don't Have a Choice

The purpose of this book is to show how you can do less in order to make more in business and your personal life. I've used real estate as one of several examples partly because it's a good one and partly because I know it so well. Since I have a thirty-five-year background in real estate, I feel I'd be remiss if I didn't take this example a step further and make the case for why you should consider it as part of your life, no matter what your primary business is. I'll make the case in this chapter, and in the next, where I'll get into some specific numbers and compare it to other businesses, including several of my own.

I train ordinary people from all walks of life from all over North America and elsewhere on how to buy and sell houses without using their own money or credit. I've been doing this for about twenty-eight years and have created hundreds, if not thousands, of millionaires. Gosh knows how many people those folks have touched and how many generations deep the effect is by now. I continue to train people, first because I love it (the minute I don't, I'll quit), and second, because I can have such an impact on the lives of folks who need a vehicle to get them where they want to go in life.

My students come from the highest professional levels. Most high-income people sooner or later realize they need something other than their occupation in order to provide for their future. I get chiropractors, doctors, dentists, attorneys, CPAs, engineers, contractors, technicians, teachers, truck drivers, sales people, business owners—people from most every profession and age group. All, sooner or later, come to the same conclusion: when they stop working, their incomes stop, too. Regardless of your profession or status, you should take a hard look at how real estate can benefit you. Take a little time and effort to explore it, and at the end of this chapter, I'll direct you to several sources for free information.

In this book, you'll see several letters from former students of mine, all of whom have been doing quite well after deciding to learn more about real estate. Why? Well, the benefits of real estate are many. Let's look at a few here:

- **There is no capital investment.** With real estate, you'll have an investment in your education, one way or another, but it doesn't take money to buy. In fact, the biggest myth about real estate is you must have capital to invest. Absolutely and totally not true. The minute you write a check, you can lose the check. Don't write check, can't lose check—it's not rocket science. We don't write checks to buy houses. We can buy all the houses we want without dipping into our bank accounts or going down to the bank to borrow money and jeopardizing all of our assets and our credit.

- **It doesn't require credit.** There are four rules on Planet Ron: (1) Don't write checks (for the reasons stated above). (2) Don't guarantee debt. The minute you guarantee debt, you risk your credit, your assets—and your marriage. Why risk that when you can quickly learn how to buy all you want risk-free? (3) Don't make promises you can't keep. If we don't make them, then we don't have to keep them. (4) Use attorneys to close all transactions, whether buying, selling, or leasing. This way, we know everything's done properly and legally, and if issues arise, we have the documents and support to ensure we come out on the winning end.

- **It doesn't require guaranteeing debt.** If you think buying real estate requires credit, ask yourself this, how many loans will a bank give you before it cuts you off? Then what happens to your business? Borrowing money and guaranteeing debt are the biggest mistakes you can make in real estate, bar none, and they've left endless people in bankruptcy court. We do not guarantee debt, period—no exceptions.

- **There are extremely low operating costs.** In real estate, you don't have the operating costs of many other businesses, which I'll discuss in more detail in the next chapter. My most successful students run their businesses with total operating costs somewhere around $1,000 to $2,000 a month, plus, of course, whatever they want to take out for themselves. At some point, many expand by getting an office and personal assistant and more overhead, but by that time, a large six- or seven-figure income is supporting it. Many run their business from home and never get an outside office. You get to choose your growth rate, tolerance for overhead, and lifestyle. At my restaurant, the monthly bills are about $80,000, and we can only feed so many people. At Global, the weekly payroll exceeds $30,000.

- **There is endless demand.** Demand for our product (houses) never stops. People will always need places to live. There will always be people who need to sell them and others who need to buy them—in good times and bad times, for as long as humans live in houses. It's not a fad. Whether we're at war, have high or low interest rates, a buyers' or sellers' market, good times or recession, the Dow Jones up or down—houses will always have a market. When I started, in 1982, interest rates were at 18 percent, yet somehow I bought and sold twenty-three houses my first year, clueless about what I was doing. Since then, I've been through five cycles and never had a year when I couldn't buy all the houses I wanted. Times change, techniques change, laws change, but the American dream of homeownership doesn't.

- **Rents rise.** As with every other commodity, prices fluctuate in real estate, but not only do rents never decline, they usually go up. The 2008 recession took away a lot of equity in a lot of real estate, including mine. But it did not change the rents. In fact, if anything, it created more demand for housing from the millions who lost their houses to foreclosure. Unless my objective was to sell a particular house at that exact time, the deflation did not hurt my investment. While other people were losing serious money in the stock market, 401(k)s, and IRAs because all assets were devalued, my houses kept churning out money. When I look at a house, I don't see a building but a mutual fund that happens to have windows and doors.

- **It is tax-free income.** All of your deals can be done legally within your Roth IRA, which means you never pay taxes on the gain. The trick is to learn how to buy, sell, or hold real estate without using your money or credit and then to leverage that same knowledge so you can do this with your IRA. It must be a self-directed account—one where you make the decisions, not the IRA administrator (consider www.questira.com and www.trustetc.com—both get what we do and cater to real estate-minded clients). Don't confuse contributions with profits. The maximum annual contribution is now about $6,000 a year. Who cares? You won't live long enough to get rich with contributions. What matters is that there's no limit on how much profit your IRA can make in a year.

Recently, through my IRA, I put up a $100 deposit to bind a contract to lease-option a house from a seller. The deal involved nothing down, a three-year term, a monthly rent of $1,500, and an option to buy for $280,000. Within two weeks, I found a family that needed a home and a year or so to get their credit back in shape, so they could get a loan. They had $25,000 to put down and could pay $1,800 a month until they got financing. I sublease-optioned the house to them for $305,000, with a $25,000 option deposit at $1,800 a month for two years. My IRA put up $100 and got back

$25,000 in two weeks, plus it collects $300 more each month than it pays, and the buyers are responsible for 100 percent of repairs. If the sublease option runs two years, that's $300 times twenty-four months ($7,200) plus the $25,000 deposit going into my IRA—all from a $100 investment, without taxes, risk, credit, or money. My contributions are irrelevant. My profit isn't.

- **It can be part-time work.** Anyone can be in the real estate business, and almost all of my students start part-time. In fact, if they can't do it part-time, they won't do it full-time either, because it's not about time. With the systems we have set up, almost everything is done for our students. In fact, I maintain, the more time you spend in your business, the less money you'll make. Too much time leads you into minutia and you doing daily all of the stupid stuff that doesn't matter and certainly doesn't make money. In real estate, you can have a part-time business with a full-time income, while building wealth and retirement security simultaneously.

- **There is tremendous cash flow.** There are three avenues of income the way we do real estate. The first is the upfront deposit or down payment we receive when we sell a house on terms. The second is the monthly cash flow we receive from the difference between what we collect and what we pay. The third is when the property is cashed out by the tenant-buyer. There's usually a backend payday from the free equity we got when we bought the house. My example above had none. I paid retail price and sold above retail because I offered terms and time. In my world, we buy two types of properties.

First is what I call "ugly houses," which is a synonym for all-cash deals. All-cash deals have to come in well below market, or we won't touch them. The second is the "pretty house" business, which is a synonym for buying houses on terms. We work with sellers who will accept terms—lease option or owner financing—so we can offer the same property with terms to the marketplace. We usually get in with no money out of our pocket. If the deal does require a little money, we quickly recapture it from the tenant-buyer because we always collect more getting out than we do getting in. This is our original payday. The minimum amount of profit I want any of my people to make is $10,000 per deal, and many of them make a lot more than that.

In fact, I won't even look at a deal if it only nets $10,000. In the pretty house business, we deal with beautiful homes in beautiful neighborhoods with no upper price range—all without risk, since our only investment is a $100 earnest money deposit. We get in, and we get out, without the costly entanglements most people think are involved in real estate. We can wholesale a house, quickly flip it to another investor for $10,000 or more in profit, or we can buy the house. Buying it means we generally have to raise the money through private lenders, ordinary people, and then rehab it and retail it to the end consumers who are going to live in it. The minimum profit I'd expect my students to make on that kind of a deal is $50,000. I have students doing twenty-five to thirty-five of those per year. You do the math.

- **There's a small learning curve.** Yes, you must learn the proper way to do real estate. It will require some time and money, but compared to the training most professionals go through, it's insignificant. A neurosurgeon in my last class spent twelve years in school. Today, he works seventy hours per week and is on call twenty-four hours a day. His income used to be around $700,000 a year. Now, it's down to $250,000 because of government interference. He came to me, looking for a way to replace his business. Can you imagine a neurosurgeon looking for a way out? Most of my students are up and running, well versed, and doing extremely well within their first year. Some make as much as or more than our neurosurgeon in their second year— and they're building an empire while doing it.

- **You can work with family . . . or not.** You can work with your spouse or other family members and get them involved in the business, or not. To be honest, I don't work with my wife. Perhaps that's why we just celebrated our fiftieth anniversary. However, a lot of couples come through our training and are very happy working together. You get to choose. I also have couples who have two real estate businesses running simultaneously and divide the labor, so they don't actually work too closely together.

All right, I know you're asking, "Why do I need real estate when I already have a business or a profession?" Well, first of all, you might as well get to know real estate because it's going to be with you for eternity. Today, you live and work in it. When you die, you'll either be buried under it or spread over it, so you better get to know it. Second, show me a super wealthy person who doesn't own real estate. Maybe they didn't use real estate to get rich, but when they become rich, most buy real estate in residential or commercial form. What do they know that perhaps you should take the time to learn?

I buy real estate without money, and so do my students. But sometimes, I use money, and the returns are just outrageous compared to any other investment. For example, I buy two or three houses per month for all cash at somewhere between 40 and 50 percent of their after-repaired value. Let's just assume I paid $50,000 for a property needing $25,000 of work. It was worth about $125,000 after it was fixed, on the low end of the spectrum. Let's just say I wrote that initial check for $50,000 to buy the property. Now, within thirty days, I decided I didn't want to do the rehab, so I flipped the property for $60,000. I only netted $10,000, but let's look at this on an annual rate of return. Yes, $10,000 is 20 percent of $50,000, but I got my $10,000 in one month; therefore, my annual rate of return is 20 percent times twelve, or a 240 percent annual rate of return on my money.

Show me a stock where you can make a 240 percent annual rate return in one month and never put up money or own it. And if, as I recommended above, you do this deal within your Roth IRA, you'll pay no taxes on it. I can tell you, by the way, the government is looking to make a mess out of this opportunity and collect money from people who have literally billions of dollars sitting in IRAs across America. The lesson here is, get in while the getting's good.

Real estate is a wealth-creating vehicle, which all people need, regardless of their professions. No matter what you do or how much money you're making, there's going to come a time when you don't want to do it anymore. And even if you're doing well, ask yourself, "Okay, what about retirement?" Yes, if you have a lot of cash coming in, there are a lot of things you can do with it. I'll be the first to tell you, cash is easier to manage than properties, but I'd like to explode the myth that managing properties is a big deal.

Please note: every time I put lease-option tenant-buyers in one of my homes, 100 percent of the responsibility for repairs passes onto them. I don't do repairs. And every time I turn over the keys, the tenant-buyers have given me thousands of dollars in the form of a nonrefundable option deposit. These folks aren't tenants. They're tenant-buyers, with a totally different attitude. They don't create the problems tenants create. I don't unplug their toilets. They don't call me in the middle of the night. In fact, they don't call me at all.

This is a higher level of real estate investing. It allows us to eliminate all the issues that follow tenants who can barely come up with enough money for deposits, much less rent. My folks have skin in the game. When they move, they leave the deposit behind, and they don't expect to get it back. So they act differently and think differently than tenants. They pay down our debt while the property is increasing in value. If they buy, they buy. If they don't buy, they don't buy. Frankly, I don't care which, because as long as they're in the house, I'm keeping the golden goose alive. It just keeps laying golden eggs, getting better every single month.

Real estate is an IDEAL investment:

    I   is for the interest we get to collect.

    D   is for our ability to depreciate the asset, which we generally get for free.

    E   is for the free equity we almost always get.

    A   is for appreciation, meaning property values rise.

    L   is for leverage. We can control millions in assets without investing capital.

No other type of investment can be leveraged like real estate. Almost all the deals we do are transacted without any of our capital, so we have 100 percent leverage. There's no need to go to the bank, because we buy with owner financing—usually with no money down—or with lease purchasing and nothing down. Real estate is not a place to put money—it's an asset that generates cash. We get the real estate for free, and then we turn it into cash. We then decide what to do with that cash to grow it while our real estate is producing more cash.

However, real estate is also a place to put cash, as long as it isn't buried there long term. You'll never get a better rate of return semipassively than by using cash to buy real estate—but only if the intent is to get that cash back quickly with more cash. I won't cover this common mistake here, but I will if we ever get together in a classroom. On Planet Ron, we don't leave our money in real estate, which is what conventional wisdom wants you to do when you put up a 20 percent down payment to buy a property.

I think I've already made the case, but since so many people fear it—and rightfully so—let me emphasize again, management is not a problem when you do real estate Ron's way. Putting lease-option tenant-buyers with skin in the game in houses eliminates all sorts of headaches. At one time, I had 276 rental units, and more than two hundred of them were Section 8 HUD tenants. That's real management. I used to have dark hair. I lost it during the years in which I owned all of those low-end rental units.

It took me a long time to get out of the mess I created in my first few years of business, thinking tenants in houses would make me rich. Of course, they can, but you have to go through an awful lot to get rich that way. No one tells you how much of your life it's going to suck up. I love tenants . . . as long as they're doing their own repairs and have given me thousands of dollars. I hate tenants when they expect me to fix all of the petty problems in their lives and don't keep their promises.

Real estate the way we do it requires less time and patience. It doesn't require a license either. We have a lot of licensed people in our industry, which is fine, but what we do doesn't require one. You'll make more as a real estate investor than you will as a real estate agent, but I have no problem with people combining the two. I have a lot of students doing just that.

The question really is, "Why wouldn't you want to learn about real estate and enjoy all the benefits we've just discussed?" One of the biggest is cash flow. I have a long list of people who net seven figures annually doing what we teach. Of course, the list of folks who are netting six figures is many times as long. They make way more than they ever received in their jobs, and in the process, have recaptured their lives and taken back their time. The way things can be systemized today, they have almost nothing to do except make decisions.

Here are some resources that will provide more information about real estate investing for free. You'll find my book, *How to Be a Quick Turn Real Estate Millionaire* at www.RonsFreeBook.com. I have a course on wholesaling (putting ugly houses under contract and then flipping them to investors) available for a dollar, at www.RonsDollarDeal.com. You can download that $599 course for a dollar as long as you opt into our Gold Club, which is the biggest bargain in real estate today. You must say yes to opting in, but you have a thirty-day trial during which you can opt out. It's only $59 a month if you stay. The benefits of the Gold Club site are enormous, with more than two hundred hours of instruction. You also have access to all of my forms and agreements from all my courses to use whenever you need them while running your business.

If you want to learn about my four-day training, which as of this writing I still teach, Google "quick start real estate school" to find the page, or call our office at 800-567-6128. Go online and take a look, but I suggest you call rather than order on the web. You'll get a discount if you call our office and say you got the number from this book. My main website is www.RonLegrand.com. There, you can get all kinds of goodies, information, and a schedule of where we'll be. The website also lists all the courses available to help you get started and to learn from the most qualified guy alive how to buy and sell houses without using your money or credit, period (he's very modest, too).

CHAPTER 10

Real Estate Ron's Way

Automation Keeps Costs Low, Profits High, and Kills Minutia

In chapter 5, we covered the five steps any business must take to operate. These five steps are the same whether you're in retail, service, medicine, dining, consulting, or another business, but now I'd like to demonstrate how I work through these steps in my real estate business. It's a good illustration because I've mastered it, and everyone can relate to real estate, whether you've already invested in it or will soon.

The first step for any business is to locate prospects. In my real estate business, I have my VAs generate prospects by calling ads that run online. I also do a few things to generate leads myself from FSBOs, and I have the VAs follow up with calls to those owners. One of these things is mailing letters to targeted FSBOs. That's done by www.YellowLetterLady.com. We simply order the number of letters to be sent, designate a particular list, and say when to mail them. All the inbound calls go to a twenty-four-hour answering service, www.PatLive.com/RonLeGrand.com. The service forwards them to us, and we send them to the VAs to call.

Through Craigslist ads, we get field agents who'll ride around and take pictures of FSBO signs in front of houses. The field agents send us the pictures, which are forwarded to the VAs, who call the numbers on the signs. This gets us an enormous amount of leads. Our VAs also run ads online that say I buy houses. The calls go to PATLive, and the email replies go to our website, which captures the same info as PATLive. VAs then call these sellers from info taken through the calls and emails. We do a few other things, too, but these are the big ones. Please note the letters "VA" pop up frequently.

The second thing all businesses must do is prescreen prospects. How do we do this? While VAs are calling sellers and filling out property sheets, they use my scripts to ask them if they would consider terms. All of the front-end chasing and grunt work is done before I ever get into the picture. By the time I get prospects, they've already said yes they'd consider terms, or no they wouldn't. About a third say yes when properly asked. Otherwise, they don't get a second glance.

I then construct offers, step three for all businesses, by having someone who is not on my payroll call all those who'll consider terms. My callers read the scripts I've created, and in reality, the sellers make me the offers. We read questions. They answer the questions, and thereby, tell us what kinds of terms they will accept. For example, one of the questions is, "May I assume you will sell with nothing down?" If the answer comes back yes, I know we've got a seller who's flexible. And by the way, you'd be surprised how many people will say yes and sell with nothing down if they're asked properly. About a third say yes to owner financing.

Eagle VA Service	$397 a month.
(includes website, IVR, texting, emailing, database, Gold Club membership, five hours VA service)	
Signs when selling	$25 a month
Phone and gas	$0
(They don't count—it's money you're spending anyway).	
Miscellaneous	$100

These core items add up to $571. To this, you can add the cost of any marketing you want to try, such as mailing Yellow Letters or buying pay-per-click ads, but all told, you'll still be spending less than $2,000 a month. There is no comparison between this business and a "regular" business like my restaurant. For example, the gas bill to run the range in my restaurant's kitchen costs more than all of the monthly operating costs for my real estate business combined. At Global Publishing, our electric bill or phone bill is higher than the entire cost of operating my real estate business. I guess you can see why I'm partial to real estate. It's been good to me my entire life—not that I don't maintain other businesses and multiple streams of income.

It's obvious this is only a part-time venture—I'm not even going to call it a "job"—though it produces massive full-time income. My students ask all the time, "Should I quit my job?" My answer is always no. You never want to cut off the income stream that sustains life until you've replaced it with something you can depend on. When this happens, and it can happen rather quickly, then you can decide if you want to quit your job but not a minute before. You've put up with it this long. Put up with it a little longer.

Limited time is a reason to get into real estate, not an excuse to avoid it. I tell people frequently, if you're spending more than five to ten hours a week on real estate, you're wasting it on foolish work that doesn't accomplish anything. If this sounds complicated, I understand. This book is not about real estate or meant to be a course on it.

But those who want to learn more about real estate investing can find my mentoring site at www.MyMentoringMillionaires.com. You can get a free book that delivers a seminar in print at www.RonsFreeBook.com, and more information is available at www.RonLeGrand.com and www.RonsGoldClub.com. For a course on wholesaling houses with no money or credit, go to www.ronsdollardeal.com. You can download the course for $1. That's right, one buck. If you stay on the site after you order, you can get a killer deal on a couple of other courses, too.

Now you're probably wondering, "Well, what does Ron's approach to real estate have to do with me? I'm not in the real estate business, and I'm not sure I ever want to be." Well, if you're in business—any business—my approach applies to you. Let's consider a service business, like a medical practice. Most doctors I meet are pretty systemized already and have already decided their time needs to be spent with their patients. If that's you, congratulations. But I'll bet there are a whole lot of things you still work on which you shouldn't be doing. If that's the case, maybe it's time to create a list of all the things you do and quickly delegate the ones you don't have to do.

If I were a doctor running a practice, the first thing I would focus on, as I said in an earlier chapter, would be replacing myself. Even if my intent was to stay in the business, I would make sure there was someone there who could take my place if I decided I didn't want to show up for work, whether my absence was because of vacation or illness or a sudden change of heart.

So if you're running a business and the business can't survive without you, you're in dangerous territory—it's only a matter of time until you'll wish you had somebody who could do what you do. I teach, and I'm pretty good at it, if I do say so myself. Students ask me all the time, "Who could replace you in that job?" As I've pointed out previously, my answer is that there were people teaching for me for many years prior to the 2008 recession. I was barely seen then because I replaced myself, and they all did a very good job of it. If I choose to, I can do the same again. Yes . . . even gurus can be replaced!

Now, let's assume you're a retail store, or a restaurant, and you're the manager or the owner. If that's true, remember, your job is to read reports, make decisions based on them, focus on revenue, and supervise the marketing, which will bring more customers. If you head the business and do not focus on these items, it's not likely anyone else in your organization will, because no one cares as much as you. "The less I do, the more I make" is a lifestyle, not mere words. I'm the first to confess it won't be easy. It's a habit change, and those take time. We spend all of our lives sucked into minutia, trying to do every little thing, putting our hands into every action that has to be taken within our business and our lives, assuming no one can do the job as well as we can, wondering what will happen if we turn loose and let somebody else try.

It's not hard for me to see why most people will never be free from their businesses. Liberation is difficult, but it is worth the effort. If you take the time to delegate, systemize, and automate, it'll change your life. It'll make you a better person. It'll make you easier to live with, work with, and do business with. You'll boost your revenue and probably even your health and sex life because in the process, you'll be removing stress.

If you run or own a business, you'll know you've arrived when you wake up in the morning and must look for something to do. There will be plenty of things you can do but nothing you're required to do. When this happens, you've mastered the arts of delegating, automating, systemizing, and outsourcing.

Would you like to work from home and spend more time with your kids?

Would you like to secure your future and live the good life you deserve?

Would you like to work from home and spend more time with your kids? Would you like to secure your future and live the good life you deserve? If your answer to these questions is yes, then today is your lucky day because I have a brand new CD and a best-selling book titled *How to Be a Quick Turn Real Estate Entrepreneur in Any Economy* that'll show you how.

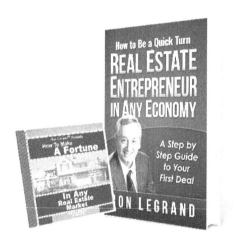

This book is making millionaire$! And it's your$—FREE!

You might think receiving a FREE book and CD is what makes you "lucky," and I'd have to agree, but what makes you really lucky is the fact that you'll be receiving brand-new information that took me thirty-four years to perfect.

My name is Ron LeGrand, and I'm making millionaires all over North America. Won't you join me? You see, I wasn't born rich. I'm an ex-mechanic who went from rags to riches with what I've learned and systemized from purchasing more than 2,500 houses. And I could do the same for you.

You too can discover just how easy and simple it really is to get filthy rich in real estate. The best part is I'll show you how you can do it without using any of your own money or credit.

Be the first to receive this just-released CD!

Not only are you going to receive my book, but you'll also get my newly released CD, *How to Make a Fortune in Any Real Estate Market*. My students are making a killing in real estate investing because they are taking advantage of what others don't know.

So if you're ready to spend more time with your family and secure your future, don't hesitate to call **1-800-869-1453** and leave a message twenty-four hours a day, and make sure you let them know that today is your lucky day to receive my best-selling book and hot CD.

My book and CD offer is valued at $99. That's right—a $99 value FREE to you. To take advantage of this incredibly hot deal. Just call, and I'll send you the information to start the ball rolling toward your financial freedom!

Can you think of any phone call you've made that has made a big impact on your life? I'd say this could be the most important call you'll ever make.

Call 1-800-870-4365 before supplies run out.
www.RonLeGrand.com/FREECD&BOOK

Praise from Ron's Students

ANDREAS & BROOKE SAKELLARIS
Lancaster, PA

"I am so thrilled to take charge of my own destiny..."

Dear Mentors,

I wanted to say THANK YOU SOOO much for all the support you have given me.

Before starting mentorship with you, I was stuck in paralysis of analysis. I was afraid to talk to seller and make offers in fear that I couldn't explain the creative terms. Now that I understand the strategies, I feel empowered and confident to be offering most sellers a solution to their problem when there were no other options for them.

Through your mentorship I have not only been able to flip my first wholesale deal and get my "SHUT UP CHECK," over $7,000, but you have coached me into setting up my business into the autopilot stage (HUGE GAME CHANGER). Using VAs to do all the back office work that I used to get drowned in (getting no where) now for me, and I can the more lucrative

business. Thanks to you guys now I understand the Control Without Ownership and ACTS strategies, which is such a great tool in this economy. We are able to do deals that most investors throw in the trash.

I am so thrilled to take charge of my own destiny and create my future. The freedom that this business will bring to my family is priceless. Being able to take this set of skills and implement them anywhere is so exciting. No longer do we have to suffer the cold winters of the Northeast. We will continue to do deals and build the business through our VAs here in PA, but come next winter we are opening up shop and moving to Florida!!!!!

We just want to be like you guys.

Overall, this experience has been one which has sparked the fire within and made me a true believer in myself. I greatly appreciate the support and encouragement from you both, as well as Ron's teaching. We look forward to growing in the business and continuing our relationship as well as expanding the endless opportunities. The ultimate will be when we are able to give back just like you have done for us!

Most Sincerely,

Andreas & Brooke Sakellaris

Lancaster, PA

ANDREW SCHLAG
Belle River, IL

"I thank the Lord for letting me be in this business."

Hello,

I just wanted to share another house I just bought in a lovely neighborhood subject-to. It seemed like so many people just wanted cash for their properties and wouldn't let me take over the debt! But

now this is my fourth subject-to deal since I entered Ron's mentoring program!

The gentleman was transferring jobs and moving to Tennessee, so I offered to take over his debt of $164,000 and caught up his sewer liens on the home as well. It needs a little TLC, but I'm putting it on the market at $200,000. Excited to see what happens. I thank the Lord for letting me be in this business. I'm loving it more and more!

My mentors have also helped me to get from dreading seller calls to being excited to make seller calls!

Thank you Ron and your team of mentors! I couldn't have done it without you

Thank you, thank you, thank you!

Your friend,

Andrew Schlag

Hello,

My name is Andrew! I'm so happy to be in the mentor program. Always having those weekly calls helps me push to do what I need to! Having unlimited emails through the week to answer any questions I have and proofread my contracts is such a blessing as well!

I was blessed to have a gentleman call me with a house he wanted to get rid of. He saw my ugly handwritten sign that said "I Buy Houses CA$H." He wanted $15,000. I asked him if "I pay cash and close quickly" what's the least he could take? He replied $13,000! I tried to sound disappointed and asked him "Is that the best you can do?" He said $12,000. So I bought it. I just wholesaled it for $16,500.

Thank you Ron LeGrand and your mentors!

You all are the best.

ARICKA & JONATHAN BRAZER
St. Louis, MO

"...most profitable deal in under 60 DAYS!"

**A big thank you goes to Ron's mentors for
walking us through the process!
This is our second and most profitable deal in
under 60 DAYS!**

We got a $10,000 non-refundable lease-option deposit. We bought the house for $22,500 subject-to and sold it lease-purchase for $30,000. We couldn't have done it without the mentoring program.

You are so attentive to us and make sure that we are protected.

We are on our way to number three and four before long!

Aricka and Jonathan Brazer

GEORGE BRICKER
Vienna, VA

"I wish I had done this sooner."

Ron,

My mentoring service has been great!

I wish I had done this sooner. I've had other coaching programs, but this one has provided the nitty-gritty detail that just doesn't come with the mass attendance programs.

If I could advise anyone getting in to real estate investing, I would say get into the mentoring program as quickly as possible and get that from Ron LeGrand because he has the reach back to support.

Thank you so much for everything I've learned!

George Bricker

CHAD WILLARD & JOHN STOLL
Douglas, MA

"No more 70+ hours at a job each week!"

Hi Cyndy and Tom!

We did it again! I got this deal as a referral from one of my previous deals!

I'm lease-optioning the house for $261,000, and I plan to sell it for $310,000. There are no monthly payments until cashed out—that means I pay out "0" a month!

Here's what I get:

$15,000 down

$1,500 a month for 3 years ($54,000)

$34,000 at closing

_____

$103,000 total profit!

Thanks to this program, I was able to quit my job and incorporate my family into our real estate business.

No more 70+ hours at a job each week!

Thank you for being great mentors!

Chad Willard and John Stoll

DAVID SHELL
Lancaster, PA

"I am so thrilled to take charge of my own destiny..."

Ron's mentors have been extremely helpful!

I purchased a house for $70K from a seller, and I then sold it to a tenant-buyer for $139,900—$3,500 deposit and an additional $350 per month in cash flow.

The mentors have put me in touch with the right contacts to help me automate my business. Connections in this business really is the key to success.

They are always available and does not hesitate to call if I run into a roadblock. Having a mentor is extremely important when starting out in this business.

Thank you,

David Shell

ERIC AND BARRY SANDHAUS
Apopka, FL

"We wanted to share our latest deal—
we are going to be making $100,000!!!"

Hi Mentors,

We wanted to share our latest deal—we are going to be making $100,000!!!

ARV: $200,000
Purchase Price from HUD: $100,821
Private money loan at 10%: $130,000
Collect at closing: $29,179
Repairs: $10,000

Sell on lease-option: $199,900
Collect Down Payment: $25,000
Monthly payment on $130k: $1,083
Monthly payment on lease-option: $1,500
Monthly spread is $417 x 24 months: $10,008
Cash out: $174,900
Loan: $130,000
Collect on back end: $44,900

Cash at closing: $29,179
Down payment: $25,000
Monthly spread: $10,008
Collect on back end: $44,900
Total: $109,087

Less repairs: $10,000

Total Profit is $99,087!

That is a $100,000 doing it Ron's way!!

Thank you for being awesome mentors!
Eric and Barry Sandhaus
Homes to Own, Apopka, FL

PHIL & CINDY SALAZAR
Tacoma, WA

"After a little over a week of marketing,
we got a buyer who called us."

Dear Ron,

Yessss!! We closed on our first deal. It was more than eleven weeks coming (of course, we put in many other offers until this one re-surfaced), but we can truly say with a whole heart how incredibly valuable your motivation, faith in us and audacity in making us stay the course has been. Thank you, thank you, thank you!

Our shut-up check is for $12,000 today and a monthly cash flow of $350/mo. for the next five years, which is $21,000. Oh, and a payday at the end when they exercise their option to purchase of an additional $10,000. Providing it goes full term, that equals $43,000 on this one deal.

The deal summary: This deal came about because of a response to a Craigslist ad that Phil saw and immediately called late one night. The owner responded enthusiastically by saying, "Either you take it, or I'm just walking away, and the bank can have it back." Upon arriving at the property the following day, Phil encountered a fairly new house in a fairly new subdivision.

The house had barely been lived in. The owner had just finished a nasty divorce and just wanted to get rid of it. There were delinquent bills, and HOA fees hadn't been paid in a year. By now, the owner just wanted out. We explained the way he could immediately get relief would be to sign over the deed, and we would take responsibility for the payments from here on out and find a buyer who would live in it.

Things went textbook like until the wife caught wind of what was taking place. Although she was not on the title nor the loan papers, she threatened to sue and go after the house. The owner somehow felt loyalty to her and disappeared from the scene after we had a signed contract and were to close within a couple of days. This is where the power of having a mentor comes in and having an attorney who is on your side. Our attorney was available if we wanted to go after the owner on specific performance. We didn't know whether it was worth it or not. After consulting with our mentors they gave us the confidence we needed to go ahead.

We had to track the owner down, as he had moved. Our attorney found his mailing address and had delivered a package from his office spelling out the consequences of not following through on a legal binding agreement. Magically, the day after he was contacted, the owner called us out of the blue. He agreed to go to our attorney's office and close.

With deed and keys turned over to our company, we commenced marketing to sell.

After a little over a week of marketing, we got a buyer who called us.

They liked the house so we drew up an agreement and collected a $1,000 nonrefundable check. Three days later we collected the rest, and they are the happy tenant buyers of our house that we got for FREE.

Thank you again for having such wonderful mentors that kept us at it were always there for us.

This has been a confidence builder, and we believe that this is only the breakthrough and beginning of greater things to come.

Sincerely,

Phil & Cindy Salazar

Home Connections, Tacoma, WA

JOSH NOLKE

Franklin, WI

"... I deposited my first check at the bank today!"

Hello,

Just wanted to let you know that I deposited my first check at the bank today!

After attending Quick Start School, I quickly put an Ugly House under contract for $46,500.

After a couple weeks of marketing the property, I was able to sell it to another investor for $60,000 all cash! ($1,000 earnest money and $11,701.34 at closing).

Special thanks to my mentor for helping me consider multiple exit strategies and coaching me through the selling process.

Thank you,

Josh Nolke

Principle Home Buyers

ROBIN AND SKIP HOLLIFIELD
Tulsa, OK

*"We got our first contract during
our 2nd week of mentoring."*

Hi Ron,

We got our first contract during our second week of mentoring. We got the lead through the Gold Club Lead Service. The whole process was both exciting and terrifying. Thanks to your mentors for answering all our questions and giving us the confidence to do this deal. Without your mentoring, we probably would never have done a deal like this.

The ARV is $600,000 or maybe higher. The seller owes $215,000 on the loan and about $65,000 in arrears, for a total of about $280,000. Payments are about $1,800 PITI. The house is 5,800 square feet with six bedrooms and five baths. The property is 2.3 acres and includes a 1,200 square feet office/shop. Repairs are needed, $30,000 to $35,000.

The seller just wanted out. We got it subject to the existing debt. We expect to net six-figures.

Thanks,
Robin & Skip Hollifield

KENT PALMER
Beloit, WI

"I have chills running down my spine as I am typing this..."

Hello Mentors,

I have chills running down my spine as I am typing this to you guys because I am so excited! As a result of your direction and encouragement to take action, I had a $37,000 payday today!!!!!!!!!

I placed a pretty house under a sandwich lease-option purchase contract and found a happy tenant-buyer who gave me a non-refundable option fee of $37,000.00!!!!!!!!

I had a total of approximately two hours involved in this deal to make that kind of money. I am hooked for life! You're going to see a lot more of me around. I was thinking, for sixteen years I worked as a Juvenile Detention Officer with a college degree and made around $39,000 per year, and that's before taxes. I netted more in one day than I made in one year at my past occupation; isn't that crazy?!

This couldn't have come at a better time, with the loss of my girlfriend's sister and taking in her daughter, I am able to pay off all the funeral expenses and other unexpected costs due to her passing. I will never forget the first day I met you guys and you encouraged me to sign up for Ron's mentoring program. It's the best thing I ever did!

Oh, I did not have the money by the way! When I got back home, I borrowed it from my Dad, and guess what, yup, he is paid off!!!!

Thanks so much!
Kent Palmer

KYLE & CAMILLE DAVIS
Humble, TX

"Thank you for your guidance and your motivation to get things done!"

Mentors,

We want to thank you for the inspiration and the knowledge we have received from you. It is because of you that we were able to do the following deal...

We received a property lead sheet from our awesome VA. We contacted the owner who was willing to sign over the property to us subject-to.

The market value on this property is $135,000 with a current balance on the loan of $106,000. We sold the property with owner financing for $149,000 with a $25,000 down payment, 8 percent interest for twenty-five years. We cleared $14,083.24 from the down payment and will begin receiving a monthly cash flow of $331.54 beginning soon.

Thank you for your guidance and your motivation to get things done!

You are awesome!

Thank you,

Kyle & Camille Davis

Dynamic Living Solutions, LLC

Mentors,

We thank you again for your ongoing support, education, and motivation to take action and "get things done." We closed on yet another owner finance deal and wanted to share with you the results.

We purchased the property for $91,000 cash. We then sold the property "as is" with owner financing for a price of $116,000. We received a $25,000 down payment and financed $91,000 at 9 percent for twenty years. We closed with our real estate attorney who charges us $350 to close. So the monthly principle and interest is $818.75 with having $75,775 total into the property. The new owners are first-time home buyers and are very excited to have their first home.

Thank you,

Kyle & Camille Davis

Dynamic Living Solutions, LLC

JASON AND CLAUDIA ZAKOCS
Atlanta, GA

"Our financial future has never looked brighter!"

Hello,

We signed up for Ron's Gold Club, the Quick Start School and mentoring not too long ago.

Within a week of learning the system (just the little bit we know at this point) we got a house under contract using the Control Without Ownership workbook set and coaching from our mentor, with whom we speak to every week on the phone and during the week lots of times via email. He actually cares about our success, and that is soooooo refreshing! No B.S. with him. He is available (almost immediately) to respond to ALL of our

emails, review contracts, offer suggestions, and give us coaching and direction when we most need it.

There's so much good information coming at us so fast, he is invaluable to our understanding exactly which actions to take that will lead us to our goals.

Ron's systems are turnkey, and he has covered EVERYTHING in them. Someone could learn and do this program JUST by using his books and tapes, but in our experience, having a mentor to point out which book or tape to look at or listen to, which contract to use, where it is located, and just the thousands of small details and insights that he provides us daily makes all the difference in our confidence and ability to take and stay in action. It is very clear to us that our mentor is on the court doing deals every day and succeeding in his business, and through the mentorship program we have access to his experience and expertise.

Using all these tools available to us, we were able to get our first property under contract for $180K (or actually the loan balance of $140K at time of purchase plus $40K cash to seller) and $1,200 per month lease payment starting sixty days from signing of contract.

We fully expect to sell the house to a tenant buyer for $239K before any payments to seller are due.

We expect to be getting at least $1,500 per month rent, making $300 or more per month on the spread.

I think we will get at least $15K down payment and will cash the seller (and ourselves) out within one year for a total of around $65K on the deal!

Hard to believe it is happening so fast, but we are having fun, meeting great people and making lots of cash while helping both the seller and the buyer get what they want (and us too)!

Absolutely amazing systems designed by Ron. We are following his systems to the best of our ability, learning new things every day, having fun, and seeing results.

Our financial future has never looked brighter!

Thank you!!

With Gratitude,

Jason and Claudia Zakocs - Atlanta, GA

BRANDON, DIXIE, & TEAM ROZA!
Humble, TX

"We have successfully secured $790,000 in private funds…"

Mentors,

With all your help and motivation to keep pushing forward, making offers and pitching private lending. We have successfully secured $790,000 in private funds to start our next huge project for student housing. We actually did this times three, so a total of $2.37 million total in funding that isn't in our name or our company's name!

This first project is one block north of our university, in the nationally registered Historical District. We got a plan approved with the historical committee and our planning and zoning department to bring this back to life as a duplex as well as constructing a duplex behind it, giving us sixteen more doors for each lot.

We are so very excited and without your motivation through our mentoring program we might have not gone for the big fish! So thank you, thank you!

The next two are under contract with the same plan, set to close while we are at the summit in Orlando. Our team is back home making things come together by **closing and** beginning demo!

Attached is a picture of our team with our first new big baby. This will bring our in house rentals or hold properties to a total of over 110 tenants. On the side, we continue practicing the

wholesaling, flipping, subject-to deals, building our buyers list, etc...
We are so excited that we are building the business one leg at a time!

Best Regards,
Brandon, Dixie, and the Roza Team!

SONYA WHITLEY-TAYLOR
Atlanta, GA

*"I look forward to and do love the weekly calls,
guidance and advice."*

Hey there,

Just wanted to thank Ron LeGrand for his awesome workshops and mentorship programs! Ron has such a phenomenal support system set up for any average person who wants to better their life from "can't afford or not enough" to more than enough and financial freedom through the real estate business.

Without my mentors and Ron LeGrand's no-nonsense, no-excuses-necessary, straightforward, frank-yet-simple techniques, living the above-average life for me would be limited to climbing the corporate ladder with a typical 9 to 5 job and very close to impossible to be rich this way!

A wise person once said "Example is not the main thing in influencing others. It is the only thing." Hands down, Ron's mentors are true examples of how to succeed as a real estate investor. They are actually closing deals while still being able to advise me about

whatever it is I am trying to do! Through the mentorship program, I have the accountability partner I need and their wise advice necessary to stay focused and on track to reaching my financial goals.

I look forward to and do love the weekly calls, guidance, and advice. I am so thankful they are in my life. I have the support I need as a new investor to do what others say is impossible! I can compete in this marketplace today and actually succeed! So far in the mentoring program, I have closed four deals with a total profit of $72K!

I appreciate my mentors so much!

Sonya Whitley-Taylor

MIKE MURRAY
Trabuco Canyon, CA

"I got a $1,000 check… and the balance due from the $10,000 deposit, plus first month's rent…"

Finally, my first deal in the books!

I got the lead for my first deal only a few days after starting the business. It took me a few days to call the seller back, but when I did he was open to a lease-purchase.

We agreed on a price of the loan balance plus $15K on a five-year lease with my payments equaling his starting in ninety days. He signed the agreement over lunch (which he bought, I might add).

I started marketing the home with signs around the neighborhood, and the seller even helped put in a few signs!

I received over sixty-three calls for the house over the next few weeks, but none of them were serious buyers.

Luckily, I hired some of Ron's mentors during this time to give me their insights into constructing deals and offering their insights. It really paid off, and I was able to secure a buyer before I had to start making payments!

Four weeks from having to write my first rent check, the seller's neighbor came by the house while I was visiting, and we struck up a conversa-

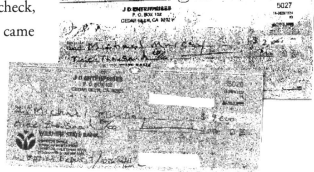

tion. He was interested, and before I knew it, we were closing with an attorney.

I got a $1,000 check for the binder deposit, and the balance due from the $10,000 deposit plus first month's rent and attorney's fees.

My mentors were invaluable for their advice and encouragement when things didn't seem to be working out. Throughout the three months it took me to complete this deal, they were amazing teammates to have on my side.

If you've ever wondered why your real estate education is peppered with sample deals and watching the experts do live seller calls and work real deals with lead sheets from students, it's simply because no two deals are alike and nothing ever seems to go textbook. So the more exposure you get to seeing real deals being worked, the better you'll be prepared for your own. The mentors are a great way to get this exposure.

Mike Murray
California

MARIA A.
Corona, CA

*"I collected my assignment fee check, and man,
there's nothing like getting that first check! "*

Dear Ron,

My husband and I had no experience in real estate, and we were living in a one-bedroom apartment, but you and your mentors really got us going!

We've now purchased over twenty houses subject-to with thirty more pending! We live in an $850,000 house, and my husband just bought me a Range Rover for my birthday!

I cannot thank you and your wonderful mentors enough. They truly helped us get the ball rolling on our business and saved us time and money learning from mistakes!

Thank you so much!

Sincerely,

Marie A.

Corona, CA

JOHN BERRY & CHRIS LAYMON
Tulsa, OK

"...we turned a 'No' into $7,500!"

Mentors,

First of all, you guys are the BEST!!! I doubt very seriously we would still be in the business if it was not for coaching with you. We learned a ton at Ron's seminar, but you guys make it practical with OUR circumstances and OUR market. I can see this business would work in any part of the country. However, I would not have wanted to take on this new business venture without your guidance. There's a lot to learn (as with any business), and the cost of the coaching program has been well worth it for us.

On our recent deal, this lead came in from our VA, and there was a "no" on the question about lease-optioning the property. I followed up with the lady, went to see the house anyway, and got it under contract as a cash sale. However, since she was slightly interested in the lease-option, I told her I'd advertise for cash sellers as well as lease-option tenants and just bring all the leads to her to decide. Within two weeks, we found a lease-option tenant who could put $15K down with a cash out within eighteen months. We explained the deal to the seller and told her she would get $7,500 upfront and $250 each month as well as full asking price for her property. She was pretty excited about that (to say the least!). She couldn't refuse that sweet deal.

So, thanks to YOU GUYS, we turned a "No" into $7,500! Thanks a ton for all you continue to do!

Many, many thanks!!

John Berry and Chris Laymon,

Green Country Home Buyers

P.S. For all the students who are "on the fence" about coaching, we'd highly recommend it. Ignorance is more expensive than knowledge!

SHERRY BRYNE
Marlton, NJ

"Your mentors have been of inestimable help..."

Ron,

I am writing this testimonial to let you know of the excellent mentoring I have received from your mentors. They have been available and supportive of me in every step of my journey and provided such wonderful guidance and suggestions each week.

Your mentors have been of inestimable help to keep me motivated. I have felt like giving up many times. But they are always there to encourage me to persevere, and they've inspired me and given me many helpful ideas.

Thank you for allowing me the opportunity to work with your mentors. I do not have enough words to adequately express my gratitude.

Sherry Byrne

Recent Deal

Sold for:	$91,500
Bought For:	$48,800
Check at closing:	$42,700
Option Fee:	$5,000
Rents 12 x $325 monthly:	$3,900
Less rehab:	$15,000
PROFIT	$36,600

TRAYE WISE
Katy, TX

*"I jumped in quick and locked up a house within
the first seven days after the class."*

Ron,

I wanted to give you an update as to my start in the pretty house business.

Working with your mentors has been excellent. They're keeping me on track and pushing me to find more deals faster. I am a licensed Realtor and have done some wholesaling and rehabbing in the past, but I was throwing away the no equity deals that I could have easily made money on.

I jumped in quick and locked up a house within the first seven days after the class. The home was worth about $135,000, and the seller owed $134,000 and had no money to come to the table. I wouldn't have considered this deal even as a listing. I spoke to my mentor, and they walked me through the process to move toward an ACTS transaction. I was able to find a buyer that fortunately had cash and purchased the home for $148,000. The market here in Houston is so great right now the buyer didn't even consider doing an appraisal. The buyer had made offers on more than five houses and was frustrated at not getting any of them. There was a Realtor on the buyer's side, and I covered the closing cost, which enabled me to walk away with about $4,400.

Though this deal did not turn out to be an ACTS program as intended, it was one that made me $4,400 that I would have passed over as an investor and even a Realtor. This single deal paid for my training!

With my HIGH energy consultant, your mentor, pushing me to find more deals, I was able to contract two more deals over the following thirty days that were even better. I wholesaled the following properties. The first one was a property that had major issues and mold. I wrote the option contract for $115k and assigned the property for $145k allowing me to make a $30,000 assignment fee. The second deal was almost as good. I contracted the house for $65,000 and advertised it for $85,000 and ended up getting multiple offers and a bidding war. I finally agreed to an $89,000 sales price, making me a $24,000 assignment fee.

You have opened the eyes to an experienced investor and Realtor for more possibilities than I could have ever imagined.

Thanks, and I look forward to the continued training.

Traye Wise

MARTY & SCOTT HIGGINS
Marlton, NJ

*"I cannot wait to see what the rest
of the year brings $$$$! "*

Thank you so much for being amazing mentors. You always respond right away to emails, and I know if I am in the heat of a deal that I could always reach you by phone. It's like you are with me 24/7!

We now have seven properties under contract, and I have also collected rent while doing a lease-option on one property (making money while showing the property).

Thanks to you, I have learned how to market and put million-dollar properties under contract by doing a lease-option. I cannot wait to see what the rest of the year brings $$$$!

Thank you,

Marty and Scott Higgins

TOM SUDBECK
Stafford, VA

*"My mentor was able to focus me and
keep my eye on the correct path..."*

Ron,

Just wanted to give you a little feedback on my thoughts on being in your mentorship program.

I know I could never have made it as far as I have without the leadership, vision, guidance ,and motivation of your mentors. I say this as a retired military man who has taught and written about all of those things. What I hoped for in a mentor was someone who had the vision of where to go, how to get there and compassion for the limitations someone may have. Those qualities were identified as the basic leadership characteristics, and your mentors have them in spades.

When I first started with them, they let me know what I needed to do first and then the follow-on activities and what would happen if I did; they were right on the money every time. It was kind of funny looking back at it how naive I was regarding what it would take to get things started, and after listening to your tapes and attending your seminars, I had scattered thoughts on "how" to proceed. My mentor was able to focus me and keep my eye on the correct path for moving ahead, and for that I cannot thank you enough.

Finally, I place compassion and motivation together because there were times when things were not happening at the pace I had hoped for, and my mentor always understood, gave me assurance in the right way and instilled the desire to keep going when I did not have it inside myself. I think they have a fabulous ability to understand and do the right thing for the person you are dealing with, and for that I am thankful to God.

I just wanted to send you a quick note of thanks for being all that you have been for me and your mentorship program. You would have been an inspiration to any Marine I ever served with.

Semper Fidelis (Always Faithful),

Tom Sudbeck

PETER CARDILLO

Beverly Hills, FL

*"I collected my assignment fee check, and man,
there's nothing like getting that first check!"*

Dear Mentors,

You guys are AWESOME! I'm so excited at getting my first check of $5,500 for my first deal—a wholesale. The seller contacted me through my Craigslist "I Buy Houses" ad and was initially asking $70,000 for a manufactured home on 1/3 acre.

This was a fixer in the true sense of the word, and I ended up getting it on contract for $50,000. I found a buyer also through Craigslist "Handyman Special" ads, renegotiated contract with seller to $40,000, and the sale closed soon after! I collected my assignment fee check, and man, there's nothing like getting that first check!

Thank you so much for your encouragement and support, along with all the great materials and scripts and resources you provide. It's been terrific having mentors, and I'm looking forward to many deals to come!

Peter Cardillo

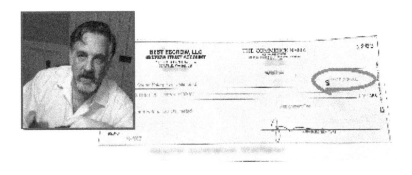

BEN MAYO
Tarboro, NC

"All I have to do is call, text or email you, and you respond quickly."

Mentors,

Thank you so much for all of the guidance, training, and understanding you have given me over the last five months.

You are truly dedicated mentors. When I need you, you are there. All I have to do is call, text, or email you, and you respond quickly. When I'm down, you pick me up. There have been times when things just weren't going my way, but when we have our weekly call, you really pick me up and give me that motivation to get in there and keep taking action.

It's wonderful having you as mentors. I look forward to our continued relationship and the success we will have in the real estate business.

Ben Mayo

WHITNEY NICELY
Knoxville, TN

*"A house with five bedrooms and five bathrooms
is completely out of my league. But I bought it!"*

Ron,

I have a beautiful story to tell you!

HOUSE #1 Wholesaling!

It took me seventy-seven days to make $15,160.50!

This is after attending your Quick Start Real Estate School.

My first deal came from your Virtual Assistants on a house that was originally a "no" to lease-purchase. I met with the sellers at their lovely home in Dandridge, TN. I bought the house subject-to with a two-year term for the balance of what they owed, $122,000.

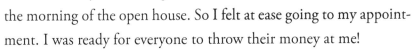

I hosted an open house on expecting five couples to look through the house. My mentors and I went through "what to expect from buyers" on our weekly mentoring call the morning of the open house. So I felt at ease going to my appointment. I was ready for everyone to throw their money at me!

Unfortunately, only one couple showed up that day. They had driven from Chicago the day before and fell in love with the house. Through our discussions at the open house I realized they were going to buy this house. I had the house advertised for $145,000 with a lease-purchase. This couple had seen the seller's advertisement for

$135,000, so I agreed to honor that price. They gave me a $3,000 check to hold their place in line. The next day, their attorney called to let me know they had accepted an offer on their house in Chicago and planned to cash me out by mid-May. Ecstatic does not describe the way I felt!

In total, I received the first two month's rent for $2,000. Later on, I got a check for $13,160.50.

I have told that story about a hundred times in less than a month. I've also told people that the Lord probably won't ever bless me like that again. But I keep praying for another blessing!

HOUSE #2 ACTS

I met with one of my sorority sisters to discuss buying her house. It is a charming three bedroom / one-and-a-half bath in an older neighborhood close to downtown Knoxville. I agreed to pay her top

dollar, $120,000. I called her, and she agreed to drop the price to $112,000.

After a month I still didn't have anyone seriously looking at her house. I called to let her know I had given up. She told me that she appreciated my efforts and she would list it with a Realtor. Not thirty minutes after hanging up the phone, a man called who desperately wanted to see the house! So I agreed to let him see it. Within the next hour, my phone rang with two other people who said they loved the house. I called my seller, asked for one more weekend, and she agreed.

Before I knew it, I had a $2,000 earnest money check from a buyer with another $5,000 promised to be paid before they moved in. Originally, they told me it would take eight to twelve months to be ready for the mortgage. When the credit reports came back, it will probably take them twenty-four months. Since I extended their contract term, they agreed to put $9,000 total down on the house and they offered to pay more per month!

I had agreed to give the seller $2,000 of the original $7,000 deposit. When the buyers agreed to put the extra $2,000 down, I decided to put it in my pocket. In all, I received $7,000 by keeping my mouth shut! My seller is thrilled because she's getting $200 over her mortgage payment per month and debt relief! Happy! Happy! Happy!

Side Note: My "bonus" on this house was a nice, new patio set that I didn't pay for! The sellers didn't want to move it, so guess who took it home?! ME!!!

HOUSE #3 Waiting on the Back End Payment

A house with five bedrooms and five bathrooms is completely out of my league. But I bought it!

The sellers signed a contract to let me have this monstrous house for $280,000. I hosted an open house on Memorial Day because I had three families interested in a tour while they were gathered for the holiday. I priced the house to them for $300,000.

Within forty-eight hours, one of the couples had given me half of their $10,000 deposit. The sellers are happy because I split the initial down payment with them. To show their appreciation for my hard work, the sellers gave me a mustard seed necklace. (Jewelry is always a bonus!) My favorite Bible verse is Matthew 17:20, which basically states that if you have just a tiny bit of Faith, NOTHING shall be impossible.

The buyers will give my attorney the balance of $5,000 plus the first month's rent ($1,500) to take possession of the house. I'm waiting on my nut of $15,000 when the buyers obtain their own mortgage in twenty-four months.

Why will they give my attorney the balance and the first month's rent instead of handing it over to me? Because I have decided that I could afford two weeks of work/vacation to attend Ron's Business Management class and the Wolff couple's Taking Action and Communication Workshop! Then I'm heading to Gulf Shores, AL, for a little R&R. Hopefully my rehabbed house will get a contract while I'm gone!

RESOURCES

StartUpWeekend.org: Not only a place to pitch your ideas and form a startup team but also a place to network and explore opportunities.

MeetUp.com: Find meet-ups and meet people in your local community who share your interests.

InternAvenue.com: Find internships and interns the smart way.

Vcoder.wordpress.com: Web design company in India.

Upwork.com: Formerly Elance and Odesk, with over ten million freelancers, recruit talent and human resources from around the world: web developers, programmers, designers, writers, marketing professionals, and more.

Guru.com: Hire quality freelancers and find freelance jobs.

Workaholics4hire.com: Outsourcing services and project management for small business owners, home-based business owners, freelancers, and people who want to work at home.

AoV.co: Agents of Value—Risk-free outsourcing, Cloud-tech solutions, virtual staffing, online marketing support.

Freelancer.com: Hire freelance programmers, web developers, designers, writers, data entry, and more at a fraction of the cost on the world's largest outsourcing marketplace.

BestJobs.ph: Search thousands of jobs in the Philippines and abroad with BestJobs.

OnlineJobs.ph: Hire the best Filipino employees and virtual assistants the Philippines has to offer!

HireMyMom.com: Provides legitimate work from home jobs posting for businesses seeking work-at-home mom professionals.

Microworkers.com: Work and earn or offer a micro job.

Growthgeeks.com: Online marketplace for high quality, vetted marketing services.

Jobstreet.com: Top job site for career-minded professionals looking for work in Asia. Employers, post jobs and find resumes here.

Designcrowd.com: Crowd-source an amazing logo, web, or graphic design.

99designs.com: The #1 marketplace for graphic design, including logo design, web design, and other design contests.

Textbroker.com: Find professional content writers for your book, website, blog articles, product descriptions, and any kind of content you need.

Capture, Store, Organize, Share Tools

Evernote.com: Flexible platform serves as a place to collect and organize your ideas and projects.

Google.com/drive: Cloud storage and file backup for photos, docs, and more.

Techsmith.com/jing.html: Jing captures anything you see on your computer screen, as an image or short video, and lets you share it instantly.

Skype.com: Free global chat, video, or audio calls to friends and family.

Livescribe.com: Never miss a word, smart pens, and more, paper-based computing platform to capture and easily transfer writing to your computer.

Building Your Brand Authority

Hubspot.com: Inbound marketing and sales platform that helps companies attract visitors, convert leads, and close customers.

Likealyzer.com: Helps you to measure and analyze the potential and success rate of your Facebook Pages.

Grammarly.com: #1 rated grammar-checking tool.

Copyscape.com: Free plagiarism checker. The software lets you detect duplicate content and check if your articles are original. (*for checking textbroker work)

Alexa.com: Provides analytical insights to benchmark, compare, and optimize businesses on the web.

Facebook.com: Connect with friends, family, and other people you know. Share photos and videos, send messages, and get updates.

Alltop.com: All the top headlines from popular topics around the web.

Fiverr.com: Creative and professional services. Browse, buy, done! Services from $5.

Knowem.com: Is your brand, product, or username available on over five hundred social networks?

Castingwords.com: Quick, high quality, audio transcription service—just upload your file and go.

Haro.com: Hundreds of journalists need your story. Free submissions!

Amazon.com: Use to find best sellers, titles, headlines, ebook ideas, etc.

Master-resale-rights.com: Private label rights to thousands of ebooks, software, PLR videos, and audio.

Createspace.com: Want to know how to publish a book on Amazon? Start with CreateSpace.

SpecialReportClub.com: Download free PLR package with content, sales copy, graphics, and more. "Finding and landing clients for your virtual professional business!"

Socialmediaexaminer.com: Helps businesses master social media marketing to find leads, increase sales, and improve branding using Facebook, LinkedIn, Twitter, etc.

Gotomeeting.com: Host online webinars with hundreds of attendees.

Freeconferencecall.com: Free conference calls with up to a thousand callers. Sign up in seconds!

Techsmith.com: Create screencasts faster with this video-editing software. Camtasia makes it easy. Try free!

Kunaki.com: Publish your CD/DVD at no cost to you. CD/DVD manufacturing for smart people.

Alibaba.com: Over one million prequalified suppliers, 4,000+ deals daily. Make profit easy! (wholesale/supplier/or become a supplier yourself)

Blogtalkradio.com: World's largest online talk radio and podcast-hosting platform. Create your own Internet radio show or podcast.

PRWeb.com: Online news and press-release distribution service for small and medium-sized businesses and corporate communications.

Ustream.com: Put the power of pro broadcasting to work for your brand—deliver ad-free, HD streaming video to all devices, worldwide.

Plus.google.com: Google+ is a place to connect with friends and family and explore all of your interests. Share photos, send messages, and stay in touch with people.

Livestream.com: Gain viewers and connect with your customers online, on any device.

Retargeter.com: Optimize your marketing spend with ReTargeter's full-service display advertising solution, specializing in retargeting and audience targeting.

Flippa.com: Buy and sell a website, domain name, or mobile app—the entrepreneur's marketplace with 700,000 buyers and sellers.

Rank Hacking

Ezranker.com: Strictly performance-based SEO—if you don't see results, you don't have to pay.

Prlog.org: Free press-release distribution service for all businesses. Increase traffic and visibility.

Youtube.com: Share your videos with friends, family, and the world. Google owns Youtube and loves putting your videos at the top!

Answers.yahoo.com: Share insights and experience. Get answers, ask questions, and find information.

Eventbrite.com: Brings people together through live experiences. Discover events that match your passions, or create your own with online ticketing tools.

Twitter.com: Express yourself to the world when you sign up for Twitter.

Maps.google.com: Provides directions, interactive maps, and satellite/aerial imagery of many countries. Can also search by keyword such as type of business.

Bulkdachecker.com: Bulk DA Checker (domain authority checker tool) provides domain authority and page rank for bulk domains.

Metacafe.com: One of the world›s largest video sites, serving the best videos, funniest movies, and clips.

Animoto.com: Make great videos, easily. Turn ordinary photos and video clips into stunning, HD videos with Animoto's online video maker.

Reallusion.com/crazytalk: Provides a total animation experience with innovative tools designed for aspiring and pro animators.

Istockphoto.com: Royalty-free stock photos, vector art illustrations, stock footage, and audio for print and use on websites and presentations.

Bigstockphoto.com: Offers royalty-free images at an extremely low price.

Morguefile.com: Contains high-resolution stock photography images free for either corporate or private use.

Stockvault.com: Search the best in stock photography, illustrations, and video from Dreamstime.

Thecliparchive.com: Large library of free video clips for use in your Movie Maker projects plus links to related sites.

Sxc.hu: Free membership to resources for designers' backgrounds, images, and photo collections.

Goanimate.com: Make your own animation quickly and economically with GoAnimate. Reach prospects and customers with animated videos online about your business.

Affiliate Marketing Networks

Recommended for Beginners

Amazon.com: Amazon offers commissions for any sales that come from people you send to their website. Amazon is an online monster and has a ton of trust and credibility. They are also very good at upselling their visitors more products, so conversions on Amazon are usually high compared to sending traffic to unknown, untrusted websites. One cool thing with Amazon is all you have to do is get people to their website, and they do the rest. It doesn't even matter if they buy what you sent them there for, you get paid on anything they buy. Example: If you send traffic to a page on Amazon selling a Sony television and they buy a teapot instead, you still get paid on the teapot or anything else they purchase.

Markethealth.com: Market Health focuses on health products, from skin care to weight loss, this is a great place for beginners to start promoting health-related products for extremely high commissions. Expect around 75 percent commissions when promoting Market Health products.

Clickbank.com: One of the easiest affiliate networks to start with. Over ten thousand digital products to promote. Various niches, from sports to real estate. Average commission is 75 percent, and many of them offer monthly residuals. Built in tracking that lets you know how many visits you sent to an offer, where they come from, conversion rates, sales, etc. Direct deposits right into your bank account. Most top-selling offers give you marketing materials and guides on what marketing is the most effective to sell the products.

Cbengine.com: This is a handy tool that helps you quickly find the best selling and paying offers on clickbank.com. They also offer a free click bank for newbies guide to help you get started.

Cj.com: (formerly commission junction) An online advertising and Internet marketing company that specializes in affiliate, media, and tracking services.

Teespring.com: Tee Spring is a great website for beginners or advanced marketers alike to start promoting T-shirts. Average commissions are around $10, but you can earn more or less depending on sales since they are based on a sliding scale. One great benefit of promoting T-shirts on Tee Spring is they give you a complete high converting landing page on their website that is built to make sales. They also handle charging the customer and the customer service. All you do is drive traffic. Tip: a great source of traffic to sell T-shirts is Facebook Ads. There are several marketers making six-figure incomes from this method alone.

Theprintful.com: Like Tee Spring, this company will be your T-shirt print fulfillment company. The difference is that this company lets you put a shopping cart on your own personal website, offer as many T-shirts as you want, prints on demand with as little as one T-shirt (no minimums), and private labels the box, shirt tag, etc. with your business brand.

Google Adsense: An easy code you can place on your website that allows you to get paid by Google to run ads on your websites. They don't pay huge commissions, but the more traffic you get the more they add up. Many marketers do make full-time incomes from Adsense, they refer to their websites as MFA websites, which stand for "Made for Adsense." This is a low-hanging fruit profit center for those who get a lot of traffic to their websites currently and want to take an easy step to adding additional income streams to their existing business.

Recommended for Advanced

Clickbooth.com: The #1 affiliate network and CPA network In the world. For over ten years, Clickbooth has taken an innovative approach to affiliate marketing, surpassing industry standards set for CPA affiliate networks, and taking their own CPA network and CPA affiliate programs to the next level.

Maxbounty.com: A unique CPA network providing weekly payments across hundreds of ad campaigns, as well as a $1,000 performance bonus to new affiliates.

Peerfly.com: Internet marketing just got easier. Join the fastest-growing affiliate network in the world, and watch your profits soar!

Neverblue.com: A GlobalWideMedia company providing publishers with industry-leading payouts and exclusive offers.

Surehits.com: If you advertise with us, we help you find customers. If you're a publisher, we deliver maximum value to your website. We pride ourselves on our ability to connect our advertisers with consumers who are in the process of buying insurance or finding a new loan.

Expediaaffiliate.com: Some of the best inventory for affiliate marketers and historically has been known to pay some of the biggest checks in the industry. They paid out over $150,000,000 to affiliates way back in 2011 and have likely blown those numbers away by now. They also offer a private label platform so you can be your own brand. They offer great support for your customers and some of the best prices.

Wholesale Physical Products with Private Label Rights

Worldwidebrands.com: Supply chain wholesalers, dropshippers, bulk suppliers, liquidators, and import distributors

Doba.com: Choose from 2,055,360 products—dropship and wholesale.

Alibaba.com: One million-plus prequalified suppliers, four thousand-plus deals daily.

Affiliate Network Search Engines

Offervault.com: The go-to source for affiliate marketers.

Odigger.com: Find affiliate offers, read network reviews, get exclusive deals on affiliate-marketing software and tools, and get insider tips from experts.

JVNewswatch.com: New joint venture (JV) and affiliate-supported product launch calendar and list.

JVZoo.com: Free to become an affiliate or seller at JVZoo. You will have instant access to all affiliate tools and training.

Buy Killer Domains

Auctions.godaddy.com: GoDaddy Auctions is the place to go for great domain names that are expiring or have been put up for auction.

Expireddomains.net: Get all the information about expired domain names. PageRank, Backlinks, availability of thousands of expired domains and completely free of charge!

Snapnames.com: Largest domain name auction marketplace.

Survey Your Customers

Surveymonkey.com: Create and publish online surveys in minutes, and view results graphically and in real time. Survey-Monkey provides free online questionnaire and survey.

Content Creation

Textbroker.com: Find professional content writers for your book, website, blog articles, product descriptions, and any kind of content you need.

Marketing Strategies
Google.com/grant: Nonprofits can receive $10,000 a month in free PPC from Google.

Competitive Research and Intelligence

Warriorforum.com: Forum devoted to Internet marketing, search engine placement and optimization, plus affiliate programs advice and support.

Thebiggestboards.com: Collection of the largest forums and boards on the net.

Boardtracker.com: Internet forum discussion search engine and analytics.

Omgili.com: Find communities, message boards, and discussion threads about any topic.

Boardreader.com: Search engine for forums and boards. Get fast and quality search for your own forum.

Groups.google.com/forum: Create and participate in online forums and email-based groups with a rich experience for community conversations.

Dropmylink.com: The ultimate link-building helper. Use a collection of SEO footprints to build links fast.

Q&A Websites

Answers.yahoo.com: Share insights and experience. Get answers, ask questions, and find information.

Answers.com: The most-trusted place for answering life's questions.

Quora.com: The best answer to any question.

Askville.amazon.com: Do you need help or need to ask a question? Can't find it on Search? Askville is a community where people love helping others by answering questions.

Mahalo.com/Answers: Mahalo's own question-and-answer service

AllExperts.com: Oldest and largest free Q&A service on the Internet.

Linkedin.com/Answers: The LinkedIn Help Center helps you get answers to your questions.

Question Scraper Tools

Wordtracker.com: Reveal high-performing keywords in minutes with the keyword research tool.

Ubersuggest.org: Get thousands of keyword ideas in a minute with this amazing keyword-suggestion tool.

Compete.com: Enhance your marketing strategy to start beating your competitors.

Quantcast.com: Digital-marketing company that provides free audience demographics measurement and delivers real-time advertising.

Alexa.com: Provides analytical insights to benchmark, compare, and optimize businesses on the web.

Trend Websites

Google.com/Trends: Find out what's trending on Google right now.

TrendHunter.com: The #1 largest trends and trend-spotting community.

TrendWatching.com: A monthly newsletter about worldwide consumer trends and related business opportunities.

Content Strategy Generator Tool V2 Update: Content research tool created with Google Docs. Discover what content is working now and find trending topics, questions people are asking, content-attracting social shares, websites on the topic and owner. Searches for Twitter topics with Twitter handle, Facebook updates, and platforms promoting the topic.

Competitors Organic and Paid Traffic Sources

SEMRush.com: Powerful and versatile competitive intelligence suite for online marketing, from SEO and PPC to social media and video advertising research.

Fiverr.com: Will pull SEMRush reports for you.

Spy on Your Competitors Ads

Whatrunswhere.com: See which ads work. Online advertising is confusing. We show you what works, so your ads will succeed every time!

Follow.net: We make it easy to follow what your competition does online.

Google.com/alerts: Monitor the web for interesting new content.

Local Marketing

Google.com/mybusiness: Google Places new name; connects you directly with customers by putting your business in search, Maps, and Google+.

Bing.com/Maps: Interactive map and get turn-by-turn driving directions. Find traffic details, road conditions, street maps, Multimap, satellite photos, and aerial maps.

Smallbusiness.yahoo.com/local-listings: List your business with advertising plans.

GetListed.org: Moz Local ensures your business listings are correct, consistent, and visible across the web so search engines and new customers can find you.

Citations

Citysearch.com: List your business and get reviews, recommendations, and directions to the best hotels, restaurants, events, nightclubs, shops, services, and more.

Kudzu.com: Business reviews, exclusive cost-savings articles, and coupons. Find the right local business that meets your needs: home, auto, health, and professional.

MerchantCircle: Largest social network for local business owners. Services include free online business listings, free marketing tools, Internet advertising.

Yellowbook.com: Find the latest business listings, reviews, phone numbers, addresses, maps, directions, and more.

Yellowbot.com: Monitor and interact with customers on social networks. Be a YellowBot Premium Business listing. Enter your business phone number to claim your listing.

Acxiom.com: Reach audiences based on marital status, home ownership, and more.

Yelp.com: User reviews and recommendations of top restaurants, shopping, nightlife, entertainment, services, and more.

YellowPages.com: Local search connects you with over nineteen million local businesses. Find people and find the right business and get things done!

Localmattersdigital.com: Web design for devices and mobile, Internet marketing, and social media, SEO and local targeting for mobile consumers.

Youtube.com: Share your videos with friends, family, and the world.
(*BH Favorite for Rank Hacking!)

AngiesList.com: Provides access for more than three million members to reviews of local plumbers, handymen, doctors, and more.

Foursquare.com: Helps you find the perfect places to go with friends. Discover the best food, nightlife, and entertainment in your area.

InfoUSA.com: Mailing lists and email marketing. Nation's largest business and consumer-list company. Twenty-four million business and 235 million residential sales leads.

Local.com: Find local listings of businesses and services near you. Get driving directions, reviews and ratings, phone numbers, addresses, and more.

Manta.com: Find great small businesses around the corner and across the country, or become one of the thousand small businesses that will join our community today.

HotFrog.com: Finding products or services in your location is fast and easy on Hotfrog. Plus, you can add your business.

InsiderPages.com: Reviews of local businesses written by people like you! The inside scoop on restaurants, beauty salons, dentists, pre-schools, spas, and more.

ShopCity.com: Tools to drive local business success.

DexKnows.com: Find local business listings, driving directions, maps, people and local information.

MagicYellow.com: With more than eighteen million businesses listed, MagicYellow is a free local directory in which you can list your business.

AVVO.com: Ratings, reviews, and disciplinary records for lawyers in every state. Get free legal advice, find the right lawyer, and make informed legal decisions.

Whitespark.ca: Advance your local search, improve rankings, and get more business with Whitespark's local SEO tools and managed services.

Whitespark.ca/local-citation-finder: Discover where to list your business for better local search rankings.

MarketersCenter: Quality whitelabel link building and SEO services at reseller prices you can make money on.

Fiverr.com: Citations done for you on a budget.

Pay-Per-Click Marketing

Google.com/Adwords: Advertise locally and attract customers with the products that they're searching for. Get your pay-per-click ad on Google.

Bingads.microsoft.com: Show ads on Bing. Display your product or service to as many as 151 million potential customers.

Facebook.com/business: Reach the precise audience you want with relevant targeted ads.

Pof.com/advertising.aspc: Advertise on this dating service with targeting options, and track your results. Over one million unique visits per day.

Offsite List Building

Linkedin.com: Over 300 million members. Manage your professional identity. Build and engage with your professional network. Access knowledge, insights, and opportunities.

Ad-Swap Partners

Safe-swaps.com: Swap ads with reputable ad-swap partners in a private, members-only site.

IMAdSwaps.com: Ad-swap listbuilding. Discover how to get 1,800 or more new email subscribers to your newsletter for free in just one month!

ListSwapper.com: Grow your list, create joint venture, and do more business.

Warriorforum.com/warrior-joint-ventures: Looking for a joint venture or partners? Tens of millions of dollars have been made through partnerships established through us.

Ezine Ad Opportunities

Flatironmedia.com: Leading email and display publisher, targeting female consumers for a diverse array of clients in a number of verticals including diet, health, and more.

DirectoryofEzines.com: Ezine advertising made easy. Solo ads, banner ads, sponsor ads, and more—all in ezines that are highly targeted.

New-List.com: Submit your ezine to New-List for massive free exposure. Grow your ezine—ezine marketing made easy.

Ezine-Dir.com: Lists thousands of the best email newsletters available on the internet today. Search, browse, or add your ezine for free!

Ezinefinder.com: Premier directory of fine ezines and email newsletters.

Ezines-r-us.com/advertising/paid-ads: These solo ads are sent out within twenty-four hours to a network of advertising sites that will email them to their list.

More Resources—How to Create a Traffic Jam

Craigslist.com: Free local classifieds and forums for jobs, housing, for sale, personals, services, local community, and events that receives over twelve billion views a month (#9 ranked site in all of US).

SearchTempest.com: Search by state or driving distance, or just search all of craigslist, eBay, and more. The most trusted classifieds search engine.

Direct Mail

EveryDoorDirectMail.com/eddm: Postal program by US Post Office (sixteen-cent postcards).

MelissaData.com: Leading International address verification and data-quality software provider offering highly customized data for your marketing efforts.

Pay Per Call Marketing

MediaBids.com: Pay-per-call print-marketing company.

PayPerLeadRadio.com: Specializes in generating leads, calls, and future customers.

Marchex.com: Mobile advertising analytics company that connects online behavior to real-world, offline actions.

Invoca.com: Formerly RingRevenue—pay-per-call affiliate-marketing company. Provides complete call intelligence. Drive, track, and automate inbound calls for better leads, greater marketing insight, and more customers.

PayPerCall: Pay-per-call affiliate-marketing company, full suite of automated telephone-billing services that help you turn the telephone into a lucrative revenue stream.

Paypercall.yp.com: Delivers more targeted leads to your business through online advertising and local search ads.

Additional Resources

Convert2media.com: The standard in online performance marketing for over seven years.

Printed in the USA
CPSIA information can be obtained
at www.ICGtesting.com
JSHW012027140824
68134JS00033B/2912